How to Read the Gospels

Daniel Harrington, S.J.

How to Read the Gospels

Answers to Common Questions

New City Press

Published in the United States by New City Press
202 Cardinal Rd., Hyde Park, NY 12538
©1996 Daniel Harrington, S.J.

Artwork on cover by Mariannita Zanzucchi
Cover design by Nick Cianfarani

Library of Congress Cataloging-in-Publication Data:

Harrington, Daniel J.
    How to read the Gospels : answers to common questions / Daniel
Harrington.
        p. cm.
   ISBN 1-56548-076-7 (pbk.)
   1. Bible. N.T. Gospels—Introductions.   I. Title.
BS2555.2.H29   1996
226'.061—dc20
                                      96-25782
                                          CIP

Printed in the United States of America

Contents

Prologue

The invitation from New City Press to prepare a "begin-ners guide" to reading the Gospels came as a pleasant surprise. When teaching introductory courses on the New Testament and on the Gospels in recent years, I had often wished that a publisher would ask me to write a simple and straightforward presentation of the Gospels in the light of modern biblical scholarship. The audience I envisioned was not professors of biblical studies or advanced students of theology, but ordinary folk who want to enter the text and the world of the Gospels. I wanted to write the book positively and constructively, and from the perspective of Christian faith, since I believe that the Gospels tell us the "honest truth" about Jesus.

This introduction to reading the Gospels deals with basic questions: What are the Gospels, and who was this Jesus about whom they are written? What do the Gospels have in common, and what is distinctive about each one of them? How should we read Gospel texts as literature, history, and theology? What special problems arise in reading the Gospels, and how may they best be ap-proached? How can we use the Gospels in prayer, Bible study groups and communal sharing, and preaching and teaching?

I wish to thank Gary Brandl of New City Press for the unexpected invitation to write this book, my students at Weston Jesuit School of Theology for their interest and encouragement, and the parishioners of St. Agnes Church in Arlington and St. Peter's Church in Cambridge, Massa-chusetts, with whom I have had the privilege of reflecting on the word of God every Sunday for many years.

Jesus and the Gospels

The four Gospels, which are our principal and privileged sources about Jesus, did not arise in a vacuum. In order to appreciate the nature of the Gospels and their contributions to Christian faith, we need to go behind the Gospels and look at the figure — Jesus — whom they describe.

After reflecting on the relation between the "gospel" (the good news about Jesus) and the "Gospels" (the four literary presentations of Jesus), this chapter will consider the world in which Jesus lived and in which the Gospels originated. Then I will discuss what can be said about Jesus of Nazareth as a historical figure. I will refer first to the project known as the "quest for the historical Jesus," then to the criteria that scholars have developed to help us hear the "voice" of Jesus, and finally to what we can confidently affirm about Jesus' life and teachings.

Gospel and Gospels

The English term "gospel" translates the Greek word *euangelion* ("good news"). In the New Testament the Greek word *euangelion* is used by Paul (see Rom 1:3-4) and other early Christian writers to express what God has done for humankind through the life, death, and resurrection of Jesus Christ. The good news is that through Christ it is possible for all men and women to experience the liberation and right relationship with God made possible in light of the cross. The proclamation of salvation present in the gospel of Jesus Christ has roots in the Old Testament. Isaiah's celebration of Israel's return from exile in 537 B.C. (see Is 40–55) was understood as a new creation and a new exodus. Thus, the gospel of Jesus Christ has links to the great events in salvation history.

The first four books of the New Testament are customarily referred to as the Gospels. They are so called because their primary concern is to proclaim the "good news" (gospel) about Jesus Christ. Three of them — Matthew, Mark, and Luke — tell the story of Jesus from a common perspective, and so they are called the "Synoptic" Gospels. John differs from them in language, structure, and theology, and so is taken separately.

The four Gospels look like biographies. In reality, however, apart from the infancy narratives in the first two chapters of Matthew and Luke, the Gospels tell only the story of Jesus' public activity and his passion and death. That activity covers only one year (in the Synoptics) or three years at most (in John). All the events treated in the Gospels take place in the land of Israel and its neighboring territories.

The four Gospels were composed in Greek, the international language of the Hellenistic and Roman empires. They all most likely originated outside the land of Israel — two probably in the eastern Mediterranean world (Matthew and John), one in Rome (Mark), and one in Greece (Luke). The Greek language in which they were written is sometimes called "Koine" (or "common") Greek — the language of the common people, witnessed in the ancient Greek papyri documents found in Egypt. The Greek of the Gospels was also strongly influenced by the language of the Old Testament in the Hebrew and Greek versions. The earliest manuscripts come from the second and third centuries A.D. They are written on papyrus in capital letters, without punctuation or spaces between the letters.

The events that the Gospels narrate took place mainly around the year A.D. 30. The Gospels as we now have them were composed in the late first century A.D. Mark is usually placed around A.D. 70, Matthew and Luke around A.D. 85

9

to 90, and John around A.D. 90. Between the events narrated and the narratives we have of them was a period of some forty to sixty years. During this time the traditions about Jesus' activity and teaching were preserved and used to respond to problems and questions faced by the early Church.

The Second Vatican Councils Dogmatic Constitution on Divine Revelation (*Dei verbum* 19) described the formation of the Gospels in the following way: "The sacred authors, in writing the four Gospels, selected certain of the many elements which had been handed on, either orally or already in written form, others they synthesized or explained with an eye to the situation of the churches, the while sustaining the form of preaching, but always in such a fashion that they have told us the honest truth about Jesus."

That is a long and dense sentence. But its basic point is clear: The Gospels must be read from three perspectives — the evangelists, the early Church, and Jesus.

The conciliar statement presents the evangelists doing their work in various ways: selecting oral or written traditions, shaping them to respond to the situations of their communities, and proclaiming the gospel of Jesus Christ in their distinctive ways. The study of how the evangelists used their sources to produce the Gospels as we know them in the New Testament, is called *composition (or redaction) criticism*.

The evangelists did not simply sit down and write their Gospels out of their imagination or personal experience only. They used existing material as sources (as Luke tells us in Luke 1:1-4). These sources may have been in either oral or written form. The study of the sources used by the evangelists is called *source criticism*.

Even the large blocks of source material were apparently compiled from small narrative and discourse forms in which the Jesus tradition circulated. There were narratives about Jesus' miracles, his debates with opponents, symbolic actions, and his passion and death. His teachings

10

circulated as parables, proverbs, instructions, beatitudes, and so forth. The study of the small units in which the Jesus tradition circulated and the circumstances in which they were used is called *form criticism*.

However complex the process by which the Gospels were formed may have been, the Catholic approach to the Gospels affirms that they tell us the "honest truth about Jesus." This affirmation does not mean that each and every detail is entirely factual. But it does assume that the tradition about Jesus is basically trustworthy and that it tells us what we need to know about Jesus. It also assumes that through the Gospels we can hear the "voice" of Jesus and know him as a person. Finally it assumes that the Jesus behind the Gospels was a real person, a strong character, and not a myth created by a group or a fictional character in a novel.

The search for the Jesus behind the Gospels is called the "quest for the historical Jesus." That quest has a checkered history but is significant even for traditional Christians. And so after sketching the historical setting of Jesus and the Gospels, we will look at the history of the quest, and consider how and what we can know about Jesus as a historical figure.

The World of Jesus and the Gospels

Christianity is an incarnational faith. It affirms that in Jesus of Nazareth God became one of us: "The Word became flesh" (Jn 1:14). The evangelists bear witness that the Word became flesh in the land of Israel (Palestine) in what we reckon as the first century of the Christian or Common era (A.D.). The story of Jesus is set in the early years of the first century A.D. in a small country on the eastern shore of the Mediterranean Sea. The four Gospels were produced in the second half of the first century probably not in Palestine but certainly within the boundaries of the Roman empire. Thus the incarnation of the

11

Word and the production of the canonical witnesses to it occurred in the Mediterranean world of the first century.

The characters and events described in the Gospels are set in the land of Israel, a small territory between the Mediterranean Sea and the Jordan River. Its principal regions from north to south are Galilee, Samaria, Judea, and Idumaea. Jerusalem was both the capital of Judea and the ancient religious center for the entire people of Israel. Jesus' early ministry centered in Galilee. And he was put to death in Jerusalem after a short ministry there.

The center of Jewish life in Jesus' time was constituted by the Jerusalem Temple, the covenant between the God of Israel and the Jewish people, and the land of Israel. Jews who lived outside the land of Israel were said to be in the Diaspora, a Greek word that means "scattering" or "dispersion." Within Israel there were different ways of being a Jew represented by such groups as the Pharisees, Sadducees, Essenes, Samaritans, Zealots, and Christians. Likewise, Jewish life in the Diaspora took varied shapes depending on the local community. The major Jewish centers in the Diaspora were Alexandria in Egypt, Antioch in Syria, and Rome. Both Israel and the major Diaspora centers were first part of the Hellenistic empire founded by Alexander the Great and then part of the Roman empire.

Within the Hellenistic and Roman empires the Jews were a subject people. First under the control of the Egyptian Ptolemies from 300 to 200 B.C. and then under the Syrian Seleucids from 200 to 164 B.C., the Jews of Palestine gradually regained their political independence under the Maccabean dynasty between 164 and 63 B.C. The Roman general Pompey's entrance into Jerusalem in 63 B.C. to settle a dispute about the Jewish high priesthood marked an increase in Roman influence on Palestine.

Herod the Great, who ruled between 37 and 4 B.C., solidified his control over the land of Israel but was still subject to the Romans. At his death, however, Palestine was divided among his sons. Since Herod Archelaus was unable to keep peace in Judea, in A.D. 6 his territory came under the direct control of Roman prefects or governors, the most famous being Pontius Pilate, who held the office from A.D. 26 to 36. Herod Antipas maintained control of Galilee much longer. A full scale Jewish revolution began in A.D. 66, issuing in the destruction of Jerusalem and its Temple in A.D. 70. A second Jewish revolt under the leadership of Bar Kokhba between A.D. 132 and 135 also failed. The result of both revolts was Jewish defeat and increased Roman control over Jewish land and life.

From the time of Alexander the Great (who died in 323 B.C.) onward, Jews were part of the larger Mediterranean culture whether they lived in Israel or in the Diaspora. The main language, even in the Roman empire, was Greek. Though Jews used Aramaic and Hebrew, and Romans used Latin, the most common language used in most cities of the empire was Greek. The Roman road system and the Roman vigilance against pirates on sea routes and against bandits on land routes made travel throughout the empire relatively safe (though nevertheless still difficult, see 2 Cor 11:25-27). As Christianity moved out of Palestine, it spread through the cities of the Mediterranean world. The growth of Roman power and the establishment of the Roman empire shaped the conditions that made this spread possible.

The spread of the gospel was also facilitated by the Jewish communites in the large cities of the Diaspora (Alexandria, Antioch, and Rome). Christianity from the first was a Jewish movement and found a home in Jewish circles. Even the Gentile Christians addressed by the evangelists (especially Mark and Luke) and the other New Testament writers (especially Paul) are assumed to know quite a lot about Judaism. They probably learned much of this by frequenting Jewish gatherings in Diaspora synagogues (which were probably more social meeting places and cultural centers than religious institutions).

In reading the Gospels and other ancient texts, it is important to be aware that their authors' presuppositions differ from what contemporary Americans and Europeans generally assume. Whereas our societies today promote individualism, egalitarianism, and the separation of Church and state, ancient Mediterranean societies viewed individuals mainly as members of families and groups, assumed the existence of social hierarchies, and made little separation between religious and national/political identities. People in those times placed a high value on honor and reputation, and sought to avoid public shame. They took as accepted social facts the institution of slavery and the authority of the husband/father not only over his wife and children but also over his entire household.

The Quest for the Historical Jesus

The Gospels portray characters and narrate events that are not part of our everyday experience. Angels announce the virginal conception and birth of Jesus. A voice from heaven proclaims him to be the Son of God. Jesus heals lepers instantly, feeds large crowds on very little food, walks on water, calms storms, and raises the dead. Though Jesus dies on the cross, he is restored to life and ascends into heaven. The European Enlightenment and the rationalism that it generated found such stories incredible.

The quest for the historical Jesus originated in the late eighteenth century as an attempt to extricate the historical figure of Jesus of Nazareth from the supernaturalism of the Gospels. The rationalist assumptions of the early questers included the denial of supernatural beings, miracles, and resurrection from the dead. The quest proceeded from the premise that the world of Jesus' time ran in much the same way as the world today runs. Therefore it is necessary to find other, more rational explanations for whatever may conflict with our experiences. The early quest was an effort to peel away the supernaturalist and mythical elements in the Gospels, in order to discover Jesus of Nazareth as he really was.

The historical Jesus is the Jesus whom we can investigate and recover by using the tools of historical research. The obstacles to such a quest are formidable. To know the full story about any historical figure — even contemporary persons for whom ample documentation exists — is impossible. How much more difficult is it to know the whole story of someone who lived in Palestine two thousand years ago! Moreover, the principal sources about Jesus — the four Gospels — do not lend themselves to such an undertaking. The Gospels were written in the light of belief in the central significance of Jesus' death and resurrection. They are documents of faith, written by believers for believers. The claims that the Gospels make about Jesus — born of the Virgin Mary, able to heal and perform miracles, raised from the dead, and now Lord of creation — go beyond what can be predicated of other historical figures.

For Catholics and other traditional Christians, the quest for the historical Jesus can seem threatening. And yet it can also help us to hear more clearly what the Gospels say about Jesus, and to listen for the voice of Jesus behind the Gospels. The early rationalist questers at least uncovered the difference in the presuppositions of the Gospel writers from those of nineteenth century historians whose aim was to describe "what really happened." Late nineteenth century New Testament scholars established Mark's Gospel and the collection of Jesus' sayings (Q) as the earliest sources for describing Jesus' life and teachings. They also drew attention to the importance of the kingdom of God in Jesus' mission and the background of this idea in apocalyptic Judaism. And finally they showed that even Mark as the earliest evangelist was more interested in the theological significance of Jesus as the suffering Son of Man than in presenting a chronicle of Jesus' public ministry.

The quest for the historical Jesus has continued throughout the twentieth century. Early on theologians debated the relationship between the Jesus of history and the Christ of faith. The form critics showed that Mark's outline of Jesus' public ministry had been imposed upon the small units of teaching and the short narratives that circulated in early Christian circles between Jesus' death around A.D. 30 and the composition of the first Gospel (Mark) around A.D. 70. They also raised the question as to whose voice is heard in the Gospels. Is it the voice of Jesus, or the voice of the early Church?

Those who claimed to hear the voice of Jesus pointed especially to his parables about the kingdom of God as primary sources for his teaching. Others developed criteria for distinguishing between material in the Gospels that can be confidently assigned to the historical Jesus, and material that has been taken over from Judaism or created by the early Church. On the basis of "authentic" Jesus material, the proponents of the "new quest" for the historical Jesus in the 1950s and early 1960s hoped to discern who Jesus thought he was and what he regarded as most important.

The 1960s saw debates about the political involvements of Jesus and his political significance, about the legal and historical responsibilities for his execution (Jews or Romans?), and about the nature of the events behind the early Christian belief in his resurrection. These concerns issued in the 1970s and early 1980s in explorations of the Jewishness of Jesus: What kind of Jew was he? Did he intend to found a new religion, or did he remain within Judaism? Was he a political revolutionary, or merely perceived as such? The 1990s have seen a renewed debate about the possibility of the quest for the historical Jesus, with particular attention to the sayings and activities that can be assigned to Jesus, to the analogies between Jesus and Cynic philosophers, and to Jesus as a wisdom teacher.

How Can We Know About Jesus?

The quest for the historical Jesus was conceived in rationalism and is subject to methodological and theological objections. Yet, it has yielded some ways of isolating material in the Gospels that very likely goes back to Jesus and thus can help us to arrive at a minimal sketch of Jesus' public activity and teaching.

The criteria for isolating Jesus material tell us only part of the story about Jesus, not the whole story. Yet they can indicate some important things about Jesus as a figure in history. According to the criterion of "embarrassment," something that would have been embarrassing to early Christians and nevertheless appears in the Gospels probably reflects a historical fact. For example, that Jesus was baptized by John the Baptist with a "baptism of repentance for the forgiveness of sins" (Mk 1:4) was embarrassing to Matthew (see Mt 3:14-15) and other early Christians, but was included nonetheless. Likewise, the claim about the timing of the Day of the Lord in Mark 13:32 ("of that day or hour no one knows, neither the angels in heaven nor the Son but only the Father") caused later theologians of the Trinity considerable difficulty, precisely because it occurs in scripture as the words of the Son of God.

The criterion of "dissimilarity" or "discontinuity" pays particular attention to what in the Gospel tradition differs from both Jewish and early Christian practice. Two examples that fit this criterion are Jesus' prohibition of oaths ("do not swear at all," Mt 5:34) and his strict attitude toward marriage and divorce (see Mk 10:1-12; Lk 16:18). Both practices were allowed in contemporary Judaism. And even in early Christianity exceptions to Jesus' absolute teaching were made. (For exceptions to the divorce teaching, see Mt 5:32; 19:9; and 1 Cor 7:15-16.)

The two criteria of embarrassment and dissimilarity can be complemented by other criteria. According to the criterion of "multiple attestation," what appears in several independent sources has a good chance of going back to Jesus. Examples would include the Last Supper and the feeding of large crowds (5,000 or 4,000 people). Then whatever is coherent or consistent with what can be isolated by these three criteria can in turn be used to fill in the "bedrock" Jesus material.

Since Jesus was a Jew of first-century Palestine, one can suppose that his teachings would include elements of local color (farming practices or economic arrangements current in first-century Galilee) and expressions that can be easily translated from Greek back into Aramaic (or Hebrew) — the language in which he taught. Finally, things about Jesus that angered his opponents and led to his execution stand a good chance of going back to the historical Jesus. An example would be Jesus' saying about the Jerusalem Temple: "I will destroy this temple made with hands and within three days I will build another not made with hands" (Mk 14:58). Whatever Jesus meant by this, it was brought forward at his trial before Pontius Pilate as evidence that he posed a threat both to the Jewish officials and to the Romans.

What Can We Know About Jesus?

The Gospels do not allow us to write a full-scale biography of Jesus or even a full account of his public ministry. The problem with detailing the public ministry (for which the four Gospels provide ample material) is the chronological framework. Mark, who is followed by Matthew and Luke, presents what seems to be a one-year public ministry with only one trip to Jerusalem. John, however, envisions three years (or at least three Passovers) with several trips to Jerusalem. Moreover, in both frameworks it is hard to follow the itinerary of Jesus and his disciples, and harder still to harmonize the two itineraries.

18

Despite these chronological and geographical problems, it is possible to construct a general outline of Jesus' life and ministry, and to ascertain the most important themes of his teaching. Jesus, a Jew of Palestine in the first century A.D., was raised in Nazareth of Galilee. He was part of the movement centered around John the Baptist and underwent John's baptism. At some point Jesus separated from his mentor John and gathered disciples around himself. He exercised a public ministry of preaching and healing first in Galilee (with Capernaum as its center) and then in Judea (with Jerusalem as its center). In the year A.D. 30 or so he went up to Jerusalem, where he was arrested and crucified under the Roman prefect Pontius Pilate (who governed between A.D. 26 and 36). He was said to have appeared alive to his disciples and some other followers, who explained their experience as indicating Jesus' resurrection from the dead.

With the help of the various criteria explained above and the thrust of the Gospel tradition, it is also possible to reconstruct the main themes of Jesus' teaching. He proclaimed the coming of the kingdom of God in its fullness and pointed to its beginning or anticipation in his own life and ministry. He enjoyed a relationship of special intimacy with the God of Israel and viewed this God not only as his Creator and Lord but also as his heavenly Father. He taught that this relationship of special intimacy with God was available to all people of good will. He proclaimed the possibility of the forgiveness of sins and of reconciliation with God. He tried to show people how to act wisely in anticipation of the coming kingdom of God. His most distinctive and challenging teaching concerned love of enemies. In his teachings and actions Jesus showed special care for marginal people — lepers, the sick and lame, the economic poor, women, tax collectors and sinners, and so forth. He took a rather "free" attitude toward the traditions surrounding the Jewish Law and the Temple, and subordinated them to his central project of proclaiming God's kingdom.

To his contemporaries Jesus appeared to be a sage or wisdom teacher who used proverbs, instructions, beatitudes, and parables to present his message. As the proclaimer of God's coming kingdom, he would have been classed as an apocalyptic preacher. As one looking forward to the renewal of God's people and trying to prepare for it, he would have been regarded as a prophet. And for his dedicated followers he was more — much more — than a sage or an apocalyptic preacher or a prophet of national restoration.

For his opponents and enemies Jesus was also more than a sage, preacher, or prophet. To the Jewish religious and political leaders Jesus was a threat to their emphases on the Torah as the definitive revelation of God's will, and on the Temple as the privileged place of God's presence. To Jewish political revolutionaries Jesus' teaching about loving enemies and not resisting violence with violence seemed foolish and ineffectual. To the Roman officials any charismatic Jewish leader who attracted a crowd and fanned the flames of Jewish messianism and nationalism was perceived as a threat to their power and security. To all such persons Jesus' teachings and actions were enough of a threat to get him executed by a punishment reserved for rebels and slaves.

The Four Gospels

The chief sources that we have for the life, teaching, activity, and death of Jesus are the Gospels of Matthew, Mark, Luke, and John. The first three Gospels present a "common view" of Jesus and so are called the Synoptic Gospels. John is different. It offers an independent vision of Jesus, with a different outline, literary style, and theology.

All four Gospels focus on the one Jesus. Yet each brings out different aspects of Jesus in distinctive ways. This chapter will first explain what the three Synoptic Gospels have in common and how they differ. Then it will consider each Gospel and treat its historical circumstances (author, date, place, purpose, sources, etc.), literary features (overall structure, plot, characters, techniques), and theological interests (Christology, discipleship, Christian life).

The Synoptic Gospels

The Gospels of Matthew, Mark, and Luke are called "Synoptic" because they share a "common view" of Jesus, as opposed to the quite different view in John's Gospel. The Synoptic Gospels present a common outline of Jesus' public ministry and passion: his association with John the Baptist, his gathering disciples and instructing them, his ministry of teaching and healing in Galilee, his journey up to Jerusalem, his brief activity and teaching in Jerusalem, his passion (arrest, trial, suffering, death), and the discovery of his tomb being empty.

The Synoptic Gospels also present a common picture of Jesus as a teacher and healer, and use the same titles with reference to him (Son of Man, Son of David, Messiah, Son of God, Lord, etc.). They tell the story of Jesus in short units — narratives (miracles, controversies, parables, etc.) and sayings (proverbs, beatitudes, "I" sayings, etc.). The verbal similarities among them are at some points so close that they cannot be attributed to coincidence or oral tradition. There must be at least some direct dependence among the written texts.

How the three Synoptic Gospels relate to one another is called the "Synoptic problem." Some episodes and blocks of teaching appear in all three Gospels, some in two, and some in only one. A "synopsis" of the Gospels prints the parallel texts in three vertical columns and allows the user to see at a glance what the three Gospels share and where they differ. Some Gospel synopses include John's Gospel as well as other pertinent early Christian texts, thus providing further parallels, and illustrating how different John's Gospel really is.

The most widely accepted explanation for how the Synoptic Gospels are related is the Two Source theory. According to this hypothesis, Matthew and Luke independently used Mark's Gospel and an anthology of Jesus' sayings designated as Q (derived from the German word *Quelle*, which means "source"). The two main sources then are Mark and Q. Mark's Gospel originated around A.D. 70, and Q probably arose in its Greek form in the 50s, though it may well include earlier material from the Aramaic Jesus tradition. In form, Q was something like the books of Proverbs and Sirach — mainly sayings without context or narrative framework, and without infancy and passion narratives. Then, according to the Two Source theory, Matthew and Luke around A.D. 85-90 independently expanded Mark's Gospel with the help of material from Q as well as special traditions to which each had access (designated M = Matthean, and L = Lukan). The Two Source theory of Synoptic Gospel relations can be diagramed as follows:

Though the Two Source theory is the most economical explanation of Synoptic Gospel relations, it is not the only hypothesis. Augustine regarded Matthew as the first Gospel, Mark as a poor imitation, and Luke as a combination of the two. A modern variation of Augustine's approach is the Griesbach hypothesis (named after the eighteenth-century German scholar who formulated it). According to this theory, Matthew's Gospel was used as a source by Luke, and Mark then used both Gospels as his sources. There are also other, more complicated theories that have been worked out with great detail and ingenuity by modern scholars. Each theory has its strengths and weaknesses, and its proponents and opponents. Most New Testament scholars today follow the Two Source theory, while aware that it has some loose ends and embarrassing "minor" agreements. Embarrassing because by theory these agreements should not occur.

Although the Synoptic Gospels present a common outline and common portrait of Jesus, they also show some striking differences. They address different audiences: Jewish Christians (Matthew), and Gentile Christians (Mark and Luke). The communities for which they were composed were in different places: Antioch in Syria (Matthew), Rome (Mark), and Greece (Luke). These communities were under different pressures: Jewish Christian identity (Matthew), persecution (Mark), and tensions between rich and poor (Luke). They present different perspectives on Jesus: fulfillment of the scriptures (Matthew), the suffering Son of Man (Mark), and the prophet and example (Luke). They portray the disciples in different ways: men of "little faith" (Matthew), uncomprehending and cowardly (Mark), and the principles of continuity between Jesus and the Church (Luke). And they view Christian life in the Church variously: God's people through the abiding presence of Christ (Matthew), life under the sign of the cross (Mark), and the Spirit-guided Church (Luke). These many differences among the Synoptic Gospels demand that we look at them in their historical, literary, and theological individuality.

Mark

Unlike the letters of Paul or the Revelation of John, none of the evangelists identifies himself by name within the body of the Gospel text. The titles "According to Matthew . . . Mark . . . Luke . . . John" were attached to the Gospels in the second century A.D. Thus, technically all the Gospels are anonymous.

The Gospel assigned to Mark may reflect a connection with the John Mark of Acts 12:12, 25 and/or the Mark said to have been Peter's interpreter at Rome. Or he may simply have been someone who bore the common name of Mark. At any rate, the traditional name of the author is Mark, and we can use that name without necessarily deciding who precisely is meant by the name.

The association with Rome is found in early traditions and fits the content of the Gospel well. The Gospel of Mark seems to presuppose an atmosphere of danger and persecution from outsiders. The Roman Christians around the time of the emperor Nero and afterward were subject to great pressures, as we know from pagan sources. Since the evangelist feels obliged to explain to his readers some Jewish customs (see Mk 7:3-4), it is likely that he was writing for a largely Gentile Christian community. Again, this fact would fit Rome well. In recent years some scholars have placed the Gospels composition in Galilee and associated it with the destruction of the Jerusalem Temple in

A.D. 70 by the Romans. In either scenario a date of composition around A.D. 70 is probable.

The evangelist whom we call Mark wrote the first "Gospel" in the sense of a connected narrative about Jesus' public ministry and death. He wrote his story in large part on the basis of existing oral and written traditions. Indeed his great achievement was to have been the one who gave the various narratives and sayings related to Jesus of Nazareth a narrative framework or plot. Besides this literary purpose, Mark also wanted to encourage a Christian community under pressure and persecution by presenting them with the example of Jesus' own fidelity and the saving significance of his death on the cross.

Mark was the beneficiary of a well-developed Christian tradition about Jesus. He took from the tradition the understanding of Jesus as a wise teacher and a powerful miracle worker as well as the common stock of titles (Son of Man, Son of David, Son of God, Messiah, Lord, etc.). He may also have had access to a connected passion narrative that sought to understand Jesus' death in terms of Old Testament texts (especially Psalm 22) and the biblical idea of the righteous sufferer.

Using the small blocks of tradition and the concepts that constituted the Christian tradition, Mark told the story of Jesus' public ministry in the form of a narrative. The narrator Mark shares essential information about Jesus with the readers already in the prologue to the story (1:1-13). We know from the start Jesus' superiority to John the Baptist, his identity as the Son of God, and his success in resisting the testing of Satan.

The plot of Mark's story of Jesus develops according to geographical and theological principles. The first half of Mark's Gospel (1:14–8:21) takes place in Galilee. In the first part (1:14–3:6) Jesus calls the first disciples (1:16-20), and reveals his authority as a powerful healer and a wise teacher, who is able to elude the traps of his opponents

(1:21–3:6). Nevertheless, in the second part (3:7–6:6) Jesus has to deal with rejection. After getting positive and negative responses (3:7-35), he teaches in parables about the mixed reactions to his proclamation of God's kingdom (4:1-34). Though he manifests his power over storms, demons, sickness, and death (4:35–5:43), he meets rejection even in his own hometown (6:1-6).

In the third part (6:7–8:21) Jesus begins by sending out his disciples to share his mission (6:7-13), and ends by exposing his disciples failure to understand him and his teaching (8:14-21). The account of the death of John the Baptist (6:14-29) points forward to Jesus' own death. Also included are stories about Jesus' miraculous power: the feeding of the 5,000 (6:30-44), Jesus' walking on the water (6:45-52), and many healings (6:53-56), along with a controversy about ritual purity (7:1-23). This sequence is followed by more stories about Jesus' miraculous power: the healings of the Syrophoenician woman (7:24-30) and of the deaf man (7:31-37), the feeding of the 4,000 (8:1-10), and a controversy about signs (8:11-13). Yet, in the end Jesus finds only incomprehension among his own disciples (8:14-21).

In the first major section (8:22–10:52) in the second half (8:22–16:8) of the Gospel, Jesus and his disciples journey up to Jerusalem, and on the way he instructs them about his identity (Christology) and what it means to follow him (discipleship). The section begins and ends with stories about blind men receiving their sight (8:22-26; 10:46-52). There is surely a spiritual or symbolic dimension to these stories. The intervening material consists of three units (8:27–9:29; 9:30–10:31; 10:32-45) in which Jesus predicts his passion and death, the disciples misunderstand him, and Jesus corrects their understanding of Christology and discipleship.

The second section (11:1–16:8) constitutes passion week in Jerusalem. In the first days of passion week

(11:1–13:37) Jesus enters the city of Jerusalem and its Temple area (11:1-11), offers prophetic teachings (11:12-19), enters into debate with his opponents (11:20–12:44), and tells his disciples what will happen in the future (13:1-37). The passion narrative proper (14:1–16:8) narrates Jesus' anointing before his death and the Last Supper (14:1-31), his prayer and arrest (14:32-52), his trials before the Jewish high priest and council and before the Roman prefect Pontius Pilate (14:53–15:15), his crucifixion and death (15:16-47), and the empty tomb (16:1-8). The account of the appearances of the risen Jesus (16:9-20) is generally recognized as a second-century summary of the appearance stories in the other Gospels, and thus not part of the original Gospel text.

In the course of this narrative (which was taken over almost entirely by Matthew and Luke) Mark developed some memorable characters. The main character, of course, is Jesus of Nazareth. The narrator lets us know from the start that he is the Son of God (see 1:1). He portrays Jesus as a wise teacher and a powerful healer. Jesus' true identity becomes clear at the moment of his death on the cross when the centurion confesses that "truly this man was the Son of God" (15:39). In the midst of near total misunderstanding and persecution, Jesus remains faithful to his mission "to give his life as a ransom for many" (10:45), and thus acts in accord with God's will (14:36).

The disciples start off well by enthusiastically accepting Jesus' call to follow him (1:16-20) and his invitation to be with him, and to share his mission of preaching the kingdom and healing the sick (3:14-15). At the start the disciples are positive examples. But as the plot moves on, the disciples become less understanding, so that by the end of Jesus' ministry in Galilee he asks them: "Do you still not understand?" (8:21). Along the way to Jerusalem the disciples misunderstand each passion prediction (8:31;

9:31; 10:33-34) and need correction and further instructions. Finally, at the passion, despite having already been
warned about Jesus' fate, the disciples desert Jesus ("they
all left him and fled," 14:50), and Peter goes so far as to
deny him three times (14:66-72). Thus the disciples gradually become negative examples of misunderstanding and
cowardliness in contrast to the positive example displayed
by Jesus.

During his ministry in Galilee, along the way to Jerusalem and in Jerusalem, Jesus gathers a variety of opponents.
His initial teachings and healings earn him the hostility of
the Pharisees and Herodians (3:6). His further teachings
and acts of power in Galilee fail to convince the people of
his own hometown to the point that Jesus is "amazed at
their lack of faith" (6:6). The Galilean ministry ends with
the brutal exposure of the disciples failure to understand
(8:14-21).

In Jerusalem, Jesus enters into debate with various
representatives of the Jewish leadership: chief priests,
scribes, elders, Pharisees, Herodians, and Sadducees
(11:27–12:44). The events of the passion narrative are set
in motion by a plot involving the chief priests, scribes, and
one of Jesus' own disciples, Judas (14:1-2, 10-11). The
account of Jesus' execution is presented as the result of
collaboration between the Jewish leaders (chief priests,
elders, Sanhedrin) and the Roman prefect Pontius Pilate
with the soldiers under him. The incomprehension and
hostility of these opponents serve again to highlight the
positive example of Jesus.

Attention to the plot and to character development in
Mark's Gospel provides the key to understanding the
theological contributions of the first evangelist. In explaining who Jesus is (Christology), Mark takes for granted the
already traditional titles (Son of Man, Son of David, Son
of God, Messiah, Lord, etc.) and focuses on Jesus' proclamation of the coming kingdom of God: "The kingdom of

God is at hand" (1:15). Throughout his public ministry, Jesus appears as the authoritative teacher and the powerful miracle worker. Yet, these aspects of his ministry can only be properly understood in the light of the cross. Mark's story of Jesus serves to redefine the meaning of "Messiah," since his identity as Messiah becomes clear only with his suffering and death.

What it means to follow Jesus (discipleship) takes its starting point from Mark's portrayal of the Twelve: their immediate response to Jesus' call (1:16-20), their "being with" Jesus and sharing his ministry (3:14-15), and their being sent forth to prolong his mission (6:6b-13). But the disciples progressive misunderstanding, and the shift from a positive to a negative portrayal of them as the Gospel proceeds, create a distance between the disciples and the readers. Whereas in the first half of the Gospel we identify positively with the Twelve, as the story proceeds we move away from them and look to Jesus as the positive example for us.

In the passion narrative women emerge to provide a positive example in contrast to the negative example of the Twelve. An unnamed woman anoints Jesus (14:3-9), thus identifying him as the Messiah and preparing for his burial. Only late in the passion narrative (15:40-41) are we told that Jesus had women followers in Galilee and that these women came up with him to Jerusalem. Whereas the Twelve fled in fear (14:50), the women stayed with Jesus throughout his suffering on the cross. They saw him die. They saw him taken down from the cross. They saw where he was buried. They found his tomb empty on Easter Sunday morning. The women — of whom Mary Magdalene is the most prominent — turn out to be the faithful witnesses on whose testimony our Easter faith rests.

Christian life in the light of Mark's Gospel is lived under the sign of the cross. It involves responding to Jesus' call, being with him in personal relationship, and sharing in his mission — as the Twelve did in the early phases of Jesus' ministry. It also involves entering into the mystery of suffering, as Jesus did most obviously in Gethsemane (14:32-42), when he accepted the cup of suffering. It involves faithful service as exemplified by Jesus, who gave "his life as a ransom for many" (10:45), and by the women who remained faithful to Jesus under the most difficult circumstances. And finally it involves constant vigilance in view of the promised coming of God's kingdom in its fullness. Since we do not know when that time will come, we should always be on guard and act as if the last judgment were to come in the next moment: "Be watchful! Be alert! You do not know when the time will come" (13:33).

Matthew

Written by a Jewish Christian for a Jewish Christian community, Matthew's Gospel emphasizes the Old Testament and Jewish roots of Jesus and his movement. The traditions that the apostle Matthew (see 9:9; 10:3) was the author, and that it was first written in Hebrew or Aramaic, pose more problems than they solve. The text that has come down to us was composed in Greek in a place with a substantial Jewish population, probably in the eastern Mediterranean area. The most likely sites are Antioch in Syria, Damascus, or Caesarea Maritima in Palestine. The allusions to the destruction of Jerusalem in A.D. 70 (see 21:41; 22:7; 27:25) suggest a date of composition around A.D. 85 or 90.

The evangelist produced a revised and expanded version of Mark's Gospel with the help of the Sayings Source Q and other traditions (M). He also sought to address the crisis facing all Jews after the destruction of Jerusalem: How will Judaism survive without the Temple and with even less control over the land of Israel? Matthew contended that authentic Judaism is carried on by those who proclaim Jesus as Lord and follow his teachings.

Matthew took over from Mark the basic narrative of Jesus' public ministry in Galilee, his journey up to Jerusalem, and his teaching and passion in Jerusalem. He prefaced this narrative with an infancy account (chaps. 1–2) that served to identify Jesus (as Son of Abraham, Son of David, and Son of God), and to explain how the Messiah of Israel moved from David's city of Bethlehem to Nazareth.

The most prominent structural feature in Matthew's Gospel are the five great speeches: the Sermon on the Mount (chaps. 5–7), the Missionary Discourse (10), the Parables (13), the Advice to the Community (18), and the Eschatological Discourse (24–25). Using his various sources, Matthew presents Jesus as "the only teacher" (23:10) and gives much more by way of content than Mark gave.

The five speeches are surrounded by blocks of narratives about the preparations for Jesus' public ministry (3–4), his power as a miracle worker (8–9), the mixed reception accorded his teaching (11–12), his ministry in Galilee and on the way to Jerusalem (14–17), his further ministry on the way to and in Jerusalem (19–23), and his death and resurrection (26–28). Whereas Mark ends with the empty tomb story, Matthew adds the appearance of the risen Jesus in Galilee (28:16-20).

In one sense Matthew is the most Jewish Gospel. It roots Jesus in Judaism and shows how he fulfills the Jewish scriptures and traditions. And yet Matthew is sometimes accused of being anti-Jewish for its negative portrait of the scribes and Pharisees and its negative comments about "their synagogues." The "woes" against the scribes and Pharisees in chapter 23 are very strong, and the people's cry in 27:25 ("his blood be upon us and upon our children") has unfortunately been repeatedly taken as warrant for persecuting and killing Jews.

The best way to approach the paradox of Matthew's Jewishness and anti-Jewishness is to see the Gospel as a Jewish Christian response to the crisis posed by the events of A.D. 70. There were other Jewish responses — from apocalyptists (see 4 Ezra and 2 Baruch), from the forerunners of rabbinic Judaism (formative Judaism), and from political revolutionaries. Against the background of these rival claims, Matthew proclaimed Jesus to be the Messiah of Jewish expectation and the authoritative interpreter of the Torah and the Jewish Law. Matthew's claim was that authentic Judaism is best preserved and carried forward in the Jewish Christian community (which was open to Gentiles, see 28:19). The positions put forward on issues such as Sabbath observance (see 12:1-14; 24:21), ritual purity (15:1-20), and divorce (19:1-9; see also 5:32) fit this setting, as do the polemical passages in chapter 23. The setting is a family feud or conflict that generated much heat — as did for example the conflicts between Protestants and Catholics during the Reformation.

Although the historical circumstances help to explain some aspects of Matthew's Gospel, its theological teachings transcend the confines of the first century A.D. The primary topic of Jesus' teaching is the "kingdom of heaven" (4:17) — the sovereignty of God that will be acknowledged and celebrated by all creation. While its fullness is future (and so we pray "thy kingdom come," see Mt 6:10), it is anticipated or inaugurated in Jesus' healings and parables and especially through his resurrection from the dead. Nevertheless, its future fullness (see chaps. 24–25) demands constant vigilance in the present ("stay awake," see 24:42; 25:13).

In addition to rooting Jesus in Israel's history and the scriptures, Matthew gives the already traditional titles applied to Jesus a distinctively Jewish turn. At the start (1:23) Jesus is identified as "Emmanuel," which means in Hebrew "God with us"; at the end (28:20) the risen Jesus promises to be with his disciples always. The first reference to Jesus as the Son of God (2:15) uses an Old Testament text (Hos 11:1) that calls Israel "God's son." Jesus the healer follows the way of Solomon (an earlier Son of David, see 12:42). As God's Servant, Jesus takes the people's sufferings upon himself (see 8:17 = Is 53:4; 12:18-21 = Is 42:1-4).

As the Wisdom of God (see 11:19, 25-30) Jesus offers summaries of the Law and the Prophets (7:12; 22:34-40). He claims not to abolish the Torah but to fulfill it (5:17). The five great speeches provide the content of Jesus' teaching, which has practical consequences for human activity (see 7:13-27).

In Jesus, God is with us (1:23; 28:20), and the Church of Jesus Christ constitutes the people of God (21:33-46). The Matthean disciples are more intelligent and responsive than the Twelve in Mark's Gospel are, though they are still people of "little faith." Peter exemplifies their "little faith" (see 14:28-31) and yet is granted a revelation of Jesus' true identity and the power to "bind and loose" sins (16:17-19; see 18:18). Concern for "little ones" is very important (10:42). Indeed "all the nations" will be judged by this criterion (25:31-46).

Luke

Luke's Gospel has been called the most beautiful book ever written. Its author was apparently a Gentile Christian with a good knowledge of and a lively interest in Judaism. He roots Jesus in Judaism and shows how Christianity moved from Jerusalem across the Mediterranean world to Rome. The author may have been a "God-fearer," a Gentile who was attracted to Judaism and associated with the synagogue without fully converting to Judaism. Christian tradition has identified the author of this Gospel with Luke, the co-worker of Paul according to Colossians 4:14. Since it is generally recognized that the same person wrote Luke's Gospel and the Acts of the Apostles, the "we" passages in Acts that describe Paul's journeys can be read as making him an eyewitness to the events described in Acts, and thus confirming the author's identity as Paul's co-worker.

The date of composition for Luke's Gospel is usually set in the late first century (A.D. 85-90) on the basis of the "prophecies" about Jerusalem's destruction (see Lk 19:41-44; 21:20-24) that seem to reflect in their wording the actual events of Jerusalem's destruction by the Romans in A.D. 70. There is no certainty about the place of composition. Greece, however, seems more likely than Syria-Palestine or Rome.

In his prologue to the Gospel (1:1-4) Luke explains why he wrote. He wanted to provide an "orderly" account of the teachings and events that up to then constituted the Christian tradition. The account is addressed to "Theophilus" — a name that means "lover of God." Whether this was the name of Luke's literary patron or merely the name for his ideal reader is not clear. Luke claims to have had access to other sources (at least Mark's Gospel and the Sayings Source Q) and to have put them into an "orderly sequence" (1:3). His goal was that his largely Gentile Christian audience "may realize the certainty of the teachings you have received" (1:4).

The orderly sequence that Luke offers is based on Mark's outline. After a period of preparation (1:5–4:13), Jesus carries out a public ministry in Galilee (4:14–9:50), journeys with his disciples up to Jerusalem (9:51–19:44), carries out a ministry in Jerusalem (19:45–21:38), suffers and dies in Jerusalem (22–23), and appears to his disciples in Jerusalem and its environs (24). Taking over Mark's geographical framework, Luke used it as the vehicle for including material from Q and other traditions.

The time of Jesus' preparation (1:5–4:13) begins with infancy narratives (1–2) that acknowledge the greatness of

John the Baptist but insist on the superiority of Jesus by means of parallel announcements of birth and birth stories. The story of salvation begins at the Jerusalem Temple (1:5), and the characters — Zechariah and Elizabeth, Mary, Simeon and Anna — represent the best of Jewish piety. The adult John the Baptist (3:1-20) prepares the way for Jesus and is imprisoned before Jesus comes on the scene (even before the baptism!, see 3:18-20), because according to Luke's reading of salvation history John belonged to the time of Israel or the Old Testament (see 16:16). Jesus is first proclaimed to be God's Son at his baptism (3:21-22). His genealogy is traced back beyond Abraham to "Adam, the son of God" (3:23-38). And in his testing by the devil Jesus shows what kind of Son of God he is (4:1-13).

The account of Jesus' public ministry in Galilee (4:14–9:50) is prefaced by an episode in the synagogue at Nazareth (4:16-30). It contains many of Luke's favorite themes: Jesus, who fulfills the scriptures and is a prophet with significance for Gentiles after the pattern of Elijah and Elisha, is rejected by the synagogue in his own hometown. This section features an extensive sample of Jesus' teaching in the Sermon on the Plain (6:20-49) — Luke's equivalent of Matthew's Sermon on the Mount (Mt 5–7). In contrast to Mark (see Mk 15:41), Luke tells us early on that women were part of Jesus' movement from the days of his ministry in Galilee (8:1-3).

The most prominent structural feature in Luke's Gospel is the long journey narrative (9:51–19:44). Whereas Mark's journey covers a little more than two chapters (Mk 8:22–10:52), Luke's journey covers more than ten chapters — about a third of the entire Gospel. As Luke keeps the journey motif moving with references to Jesus' travels (see 9:51; 13:22, 33; 17:11; 18:31), he includes from Q and other sources many teachings about Jesus and discipleship. Jesus goes to Jerusalem willingly and invites others to share his lot (9:51-62). Along the way, the Lukan Jesus tells the memorable parables of the good Samaritan (10:29-37), the banquet (14:7-24), the prodigal son (15:11-32), and the rich man and Lazarus (16:19-31). He encounters Mary and Martha (10:38-42) and the tax collector Zacchaeus (19:1-10). He provides substantial instructions about prayer (11:1-13; 18:1-14).

Though the content of Jesus' ministry in Jerusalem (Lk 19:45–21:38) is roughly the same as in Mark 11–13, Luke makes the Temple into Jesus' own "house" (19:46; see 2:49 for the preparation) and extends the time frame ("every day he was teaching in the Temple area," 19:47).

Luke's passion narrative (22–23) follows the same outline as Mark 14–15 does, but features a farewell discourse (22:14-38) in which Jesus instructs his disciples on leadership as the service of others. Though declared innocent by both Pontius Pilate and Herod Antipas (23:1-16), Jesus is nevertheless executed and dies as an innocent sufferer and martyr. His three final words from the cross show that even in death Jesus remains true to his principles of love of enemies (23:34), concern for the marginal (23:43), and trust in God (23:46).

Following the empty tomb story (24:1-12), there are appearances of the risen Jesus first to the two disciples on the road to Emmaus (24:13-35), and then to the disciples gathered in Jerusalem (24:36-49). In both cases the risen Jesus is recognized in the scriptures and in the breaking of bread. The Gospel ends with a brief mention of Jesus' ascension (24:50-53), which is recounted at greater length in the Acts of the Apostles (1:6-12).

Luke presents Jesus as a figure in world history (see 3:1-2) and as the center of salvation history between the times of Israel (up to John the Baptist) and of the Church (beginning at Pentecost). Using the common stock of christological titles, Luke gives particular attention to Jesus as a prophet (see 4:16-30; 7:16, 39; 13:33-34; 24:19, 25-27). Throughout his ministry and even in his death on the cross, Jesus provides a good example and suffers a martyr's death

The apostles serve as the principle of continuity between the time of Jesus and the time of the Church. Though they behave poorly during the passion, the apostles emerge after Easter as the confident proclaimers of the gospel in the early chapters of the Acts of the Apostles (the second volume in Luke's work).

Even Luke's portrayal of Paul develops in parallel with his portrayal of Jesus. Both Jesus and Paul are predicted to have significance for the Gentiles and to be destined to suffer (Lk 2:29-35; Acts 9:15-16). Both are determined to go up to Jerusalem where they will meet their tragic fates (Lk 9:51; Acts 19:21). Both predict their future sufferings (Lk 9:22, 44-45; Acts 20:22-24; 21:10-14). Both present inaugural discourses (Lk 4:16-30; Acts 13:14-52) and farewell discourses (Lk 22:21-38; Acts 20:18-35). Both are acknowledged to be innocent (Lk 22:47–23:25; Acts 21:27–26:32) and display a heroic attitude in the face of death (Lk 22:39-46; Acts 20:36-38). Thus Jesus provides the model for Paul (and for all his followers).

Luke's Gospel has other important things to say to the Church today. The Lukan Jesus shows a special concern for the marginal people in his society (the economic poor, women, tax collectors, sinners) and urges the rich to share their goods with the poor. Jesus teaches his followers what and how to pray (11:1-13; 18:1-14), and prays at all the most important moments of his life. His Last Supper (22:14-38) is the climax of a series of meals during his public ministry (7:36-50; 9:10-17; 11:38-42; 14:7-24). It points toward his appearances to his disciples after Easter, where he shares a meal with them (24:13-49), and toward the many references in Acts to the breaking of bread.

The Sermon on the Plain (6:20-49) and the journey narrative (9:51–19:44) provide large samples of Jesus' teaching and thus important content for Christian life and ethics. The birth of Jesus as celebrated in Mary's Magnificat (1:46-55), and the blessings and woes in the first block of Jesus' teaching in the Sermon on the Plain (6:20-26) signal a dramatic reversal in which the poor are to be exalted and the rich and powerful put down. In his farewell discourse (22:24-27) Jesus redefines leadership after his own example as the service of others.

John

John's Gospel is different from the Synoptic Gospels. John stretches Jesus' public activity over three years, whereas the Synoptics give the impression of a one-year ministry. John has Jesus journeying to Jerusalem several times, whereas the Synoptics have only one such journey. John introduces characters that are not found in the Synoptics: Nicodemus, the Samaritan woman, the man born blind, Lazarus, and the beloved disciple. The focus of Jesus' preaching and teaching according to John is the revelation of the Father and Jesus' identity as the revealer, not the kingdom of God as in the Synoptics. John's Gospel represents a strand of early Christianity different from the one reflected in the Synoptic Gospels.

The author of the Fourth Gospel has traditionally been identified as John, the son of Zebedee, and/or the figure referred to in the body of the Gospel as the beloved disciple. There may well be something to these traditions. But the composition of the Fourth Gospel is probably more complicated. It appears to have been written by a Jewish Christian author, who put into narrative form the traditions and the theological vocabulary and conceptuality that had developed in what can be called the Johannine school. The Johannine school may well have had some historical connection with John the son of Zebedee and/or the beloved disciple.

The community for which the evangelist wrote was in the process of being expelled from the synagogue (see Jn

9:22; 12:42; 16:2). They were largely (if not entirely) Jewish Christians. But apparently their theological claims about Jesus of Nazareth led to tensions with other Jews, who regarded the Johannine Christians as beyond the boundaries of Judaism. In the Gospel narrative the opponents of Jesus are called "the Jews" and have a link with the Jewish opponents of the Johannine community.

The Johannine community lived in the eastern Mediterranean area — perhaps in Syria, Transjordan, or Palestine. The Gospel seems to have been put into final form between A.D. 90 and 100. The situation of the Johannine Jewish Christians in conflict with other Jews is similar to that presupposed by Matthew's Gospel.

The Johannine evangelist used traditions that were formed and that circulated in the Johannine school. The prologue in John 1:1-18 contains an early Christian hymn about Jesus as the Word of God. The seven "signs" or miracle stories in John 1–12 may have once belonged to a single collection of Jesus' signs. The farewell speeches in John 13–17 may incorporate material from existing revelation discourses. The passion narrative in John 18–19 differs from the Synoptic account on many points and appears to preserve some good historical information. Whether the evangelist knew and had access to any of the Synoptic Gospels is not clear.

The purpose for which the Johannine evangelist composed the Gospel is made explicit in John 20:31: "These are written that you may [come to] believe that Jesus is the Messiah, the Son of God, and that through this belief you may have life in his name." The textual variation in the verb ("that you may believe" or "that you may come to believe") reflects an ambiguity as to whether the Gospel was intended to add to the faith of those who already believed or to bring nonbelievers to Christian faith. In either case, the basic theological point that is made from beginning to end is that Jesus the Son of God reveals the

Father. If you want to know God and God's will, look and listen to Jesus and his revelatory teaching and action.

It is customary to divide John's story of Jesus into the Book of Signs (chaps. 1–12) and the Book of Glory (chaps. 13–20 [21]). The first part concerns Jesus' public ministry, and the second part deals with his farewell discourses to his disciples and with his passion and resurrection.

The first chapter in John's Gospel functions as an overture or introduction to the identity of Jesus with the help of various christological titles. After the prologue that identifies Jesus as the Word or the Wisdom of God (1:1-18), the remaining episodes revolve around Jesus as the Messiah, Elijah, and the prophet (1:19-28), as the Lamb of God and the Son of God (1:29-34), as Rabbi/Teacher and Messiah (1:35-42), and as the Son of God, King of Israel, and Son of Man (1:43-51). For John, "Son of Man" is not a humble title but rather a glorious figure who mediates between heaven and earth.

In John's account of Jesus' public activity, the seven "signs" or miracle stories provide a thread that carries along the narrative, which contains symbolic actions (cleansing the Temple, 2:13-25), conversations and monologues (with Nicodemus, 3:1-21), dialogues (with the Samaritan woman, 4:1-42), and so forth. The signs include the action at the wedding in Cana (2:1-11), Jesus' healing the official's son (4:46-54), Jesus' healing on the Sabbath (5:1-9), feeding 5,000 people (6:1-15), walking on the water (6:16-21), healing the man born blind (9:1-12), and raising Lazarus from the dead (11:1-44). This last sign, of course, points forward to what is the greatest "sign" of all: the resurrection of Jesus.

The second part of John's Gospel (chaps. 13–20 [21]) is called the "Book of Glory," because according to John the event of Jesus' death and resurrection was the moment of Jesus' glorification, the "hour" of Jesus, an exaltation rather than a defeat. There seems to be a deliberate play

NEW CITY PRESS
202 CARDINAL RD.
HYDE PARK NY 12538

**Thank you for choosing this book.
If you would like to receive regular information
about New City Press titles, please fill in this card.**

Title purchased: _____

**Please check the subjects
that are of particular interest to you:**

☐ **FATHERS OF THE CHURCH**

☐ **CLASSICS IN SPIRITUALITY**

☐ **CONTEMPORARY SPIRITUALITY**

☐ **THEOLOGY**

☐ **SCRIPTURE AND COMMENTARIES**

☐ **FAMILY LIFE**

☐ **BIOGRAPHY / HISTORY**

Other subjects of interest: _____

_____

Please Print

Name: _____

Company: _____

Address: _____

_____

on the idea of Jesus' being "lifted up" on the cross and his glorious return to his heavenly Father.

Jesus' farewells to his disciples (13:1–17:27) begin with the symbolic action of Jesus' washing the feet of his disciples. This action serves to define his redemptive death as a divine gift (see 13:8) and to give us an example of leadership through the service of others (13:15). The various farewell discourses reflect on how the movement begun by Jesus can continue after his passing from this world. The principal means are faith in God and in Jesus as the one who reveals God, loving one another after the example of Jesus' love for the Father and for us, and the help and guidance provided by the Holy Spirit or Paraclete (see 14:15-17, 25-26; 15:26-27; 16:7-11, 12-15). The farewells climax in Jesus' own prayer as God's Son (17:1-26), that God might glorify him, that his disciples might be one, and that those who come to believe through them may also be one as the Father and the Son are one.

The Johannine passion story (chaps. 18–19) shares the basic outline with the Synoptic Gospels: arrest, hearing before the Jewish high priest, Peter's denial, hearing before Pontius Pilate, sentence of death, crucifixion, death, and burial. But the language and perspective are so different that the Johannine account shows little or no direct borrowing from the Synoptic accounts. The two great Johannine episodes — the trial before Pilate (18:28–19:16), and the crucifixion of Jesus (19:17-42) — both display intricate structures with their climax at the center: the soldiers ironic proclamation of Jesus as the King of the Jews (19:1-3), and the scene of compassion at the cross with the mother of Jesus and the beloved disciple (19:25-27).

The four Jerusalem appearances of the risen Jesus in John 20:1-29 show a progress from doubt and confusion to faith in and confession of Jesus as "my Lord and my God." The Galilean appearances in John 21 function as a kind of appendix to the body of the Gospel, and concern the fates of

41

Peter and the beloved disciple, care for the "flock," and the relation between the beloved disciple and the evangelist.

John's Gospel is different not only in its literary features and its geographical-chronological framework but also in its theological outlook. The Johannine Jesus is preeminently the revealer of God as his heavenly Father. He is the preexistent Word of God (1:1-2), the "man from heaven" (3:31) and glorious Son of Man (1:51), and "my Lord and my God" (20:28), the one who is "equal to God" (5:18). His apparently shameful death on the cross really was a victory, an exaltation, a being "lifted up " to his heavenly Father.

As in the Synoptic Gospels, so in John's Gospel the disciples respond initially to Jesus with great enthusiasm but often fail to understand him. In fact, the disciples' misunderstanding is a frequent literary device in John's Gospel that allows Jesus to clarify and explain in more detail who he is (Christology) and what it means to follow him (discipleship).

The farewell discourses in John 13–17 are especially important for the disciples (and for Christians today), because they concern the means by which the movement, begun by the earthly Jesus, can continue despite his physical departure: faith, love, and the Holy Spirit. Two followers that receive special treatment from John are the beloved disciple and the mother of Jesus. The scene at the cross where the dying Jesus commends each to the care of the other (Jn 19:25-27) functions as the climax of the whole Gospel. The compassion that characterizes the scene should mark life within the community of Jesus Christ in every age.

More than the other evangelists, John stresses the idea that eternal life has already begun in and through Jesus: "Amen, amen, I say to you, whoever hears my word and believes in the one who sent me has eternal life and will not come to condemnation but has passed from death to life" (5:24). Though the future fullness of life is not neglected (see 5:25), there is a strong emphasis on the present or realized dimension of eternal life. The dynamism of Christian life is illustrated by the image of the vine and the branches in John 15:1-10: "I am the vine, you are the branches. Whoever remains in me and I in him will bear much fruit, because without me you can do nothing" (15:5). The notion of Christian life as "remaining" or "abiding" in Jesus is characteristically Johannine.

The disciples of Jesus will carry on the movement begun by the earthly Jesus if they "keep the commandments." These commandments are even more basic than the Ten Commandments. They are simply the commands to believe and to love. Faith according to John is a trust in the person of Jesus as the definitive revealer of his heavenly Father. Love for John is directed toward others after the example of the love that exists between the Father and the Son. Because Jesus' disciples share in his life and mission, and thus share also in his special oneness with the Father, they continue what Jesus began through the guidance and assistance of the Holy Spirit, the Paraclete.

Reading Gospel Texts

In a book entitled *How To Read the Gospels* we cannot be satisfied with merely talking about the Gospels in general. We also need to read specific Gospel texts and to develop an approach to studying them in an orderly way.

The orderly analysis of biblical texts is called "exegesis." The exegesis of biblical texts proceeds on three levels: literary analysis (context, words and images, characters, structure, form, message), historical analysis (parallels from ancient texts, the cultural assumptions of ancient society, the use of the material in the early Church, the relation to the historical Jesus), and theology (the abiding significance and challenge of the text, the problems that it may raise for people today, how it may function in Church life today).

To illustrate how to read Gospel texts from the perspectives of literary analysis, history, and theology, we will work through three Gospel passages — two from the Synoptic Gospels, and one from John's Gospel. These explications are a beginning, an entry point, in biblical exegesis. One can go much deeper and use more sophisticated methods of analysis. Nor does this approach to exegesis exhaust the riches of the biblical texts and the effects that they can have. But we must begin somewhere. The kind of orderly study of Gospel texts presented here can serve as the basis for further work in using the Gospels in prayer, group discussion and sharing, and preaching and teaching (see chapter "The Gospels in Christian Life" below).

The Synoptic texts chosen for analysis here are familiar: the baptism of Jesus and the Lord's Prayer. The story of the baptism appears in each of the Synoptic Gospels: Mark 1:9-11; Matthew 3:13-17; and Luke 3:21-22. The Lord's

Prayer occurs in Matthew 6:9-13 and Luke 11:2-4. Thus the two examples illustrate the triple tradition (found in all three Synoptics) and the double tradition (found only in Matthew and Luke, and therefore most likely from Q). The baptism is a narrative, whereas the Lord's Prayer is discourse material. And so the two most prominent kinds of material in the Synoptic tradition are represented. The Johannine text chosen for analysis is the story of the wedding feast at Cana (Jn 2:1-11). Its mixture of narrative, dialogue, and symbolism is typical of what one finds in the Fourth Gospel.

The Baptism of Jesus

Mark's account of Jesus' baptism (1:9-11) runs as follows:

> [9] It happened in those days that Jesus came from Nazareth of Galilee and was baptized in the Jordan by John. [10] On coming out of the water he saw the heavens being torn open and the Spirit, like a dove, descending upon him. [11] And a voice came from the heavens, "You are my beloved Son, with you I am well pleased."

Literary analysis: The first step in any literary analysis is to look at the *context*. Mark's account of the baptism of Jesus (1:9-11) is part of the prologue (1:1-13) to Jesus' public ministry. In the prologue the narrator provides the reader with important information about Jesus. The human characters do not have this information, and so as readers we are in a privileged position. We know that Jesus is the Messiah and Son of God (1:1), that he fulfills the prophecies of the Old Testament regarding the coming of the Lord (1:2-3), and that his messenger or forerunner John the Baptist was subordinate to him in his person and in his "baptism" (1:4-8). What follows the prologue is the story of Jesus' public ministry in Galilee, on the way to Jerusalem, and in Jerusalem. At the baptism (1:9-11) Jesus is proclaimed to be God's Son, and in the testing (1:12-13) we find out what kind of Son of God he is.

The literary analysis of a Gospel text begins with an inventory of those *words and images* that may not be immediately clear. The context indicates that "those days" (1:9) refers to the time when John was active in his ministry of baptism near the Jordan River. One may need to consult a map to find where Nazareth (in Galilee) and the Jordan River are. The word "baptism" means to be dipped down into water, and in the case of John's baptism it has a spiritual or symbolic significance of cleansing in preparation for the coming of the Lord. The point behind the three images that accompany Jesus' baptism — the tearing of the heavens, the "dove-like" descent of the Holy Spirit, and the voice from the heavens — is clear enough from their biblical and Jewish roots. They all signify the removal of the barriers between God and humankind, between heaven and earth. To appreciate these signs and the content of the saying that issues from the heavenly voice, one needs to know where its terms appear in the Old Testament (see below).

The principal *characters* are Jesus, John the Baptist, and the heavenly voice. In fact, the focus of attention is entirely on Jesus. John is important only because he administers the baptism. The heavenly voice exists only to identify Jesus as God's Son.

The *structure* or outline is simple: a narrative introduction that sets the scene at the Jordan River (1:9), Jesus' vision of the heavens torn open and the Spirit's descent (1:10), and the heavenly voices identification of Jesus as God's Son (1:11).

The *literary form* is narrative. Yet, it is no ordinary narrative about everyday events. It tells the story of a unique event in which heaven and earth work together to identify Jesus as God's Son. Because of its supernatural elements, some scholars refer to it as a "legend," using that term in its technical sense to describe a narrative whose content transcends human experience.

The *message* of the text requires some reflection. We customarily refer to the text as the baptism of Jesus and tend then to relate it to our own baptism and to Christian baptism in general. But the baptism story here is really centered on Jesus. It is the occasion for the manifestation of Jesus as the Son of God. His identity as God's Son is the real focus of the text.

Historical analysis: One of the tasks of biblical exegetes is to situate Gospel texts in the context of the Old Testament, early Judaism, and the Greco-Roman world. To do so they look for the sources of or at least the parallels to New Testament texts.

The three signs accompanying the baptism of Jesus have rich biblical backgrounds: the opening of the heavens (Ez 1:1; 2 Mc 3:24 ff.), the "dove-like" descent of the Holy Spirit (Gn 1:2), and the voice from heaven (various rabbinic texts). The heavenly voice combines expressions from the Old Testament: "my Son" (Psalm 2:7 = the Davidic king as God's adopted son), "beloved" (Gn 22:2 = Isaac), and "with you I am well pleased" (Is 42:1; 44:2 = God's Servant).

Another historical task is to specify the ancient literary form or genre in which the author chose to communicate. One good candidate for explaining the baptism narrative is the interpretive vision found in the Jewish Targums (Aramaic paraphrases of the Hebrew Bible) of Genesis 22:10 and 28:12, in which visions concerned with the future significance of Isaac and Jacob are accompanied by the opening of the heavens, angels descending and ascending between heaven and earth, and heavenly voices.

Historical analysis is also concerned with what really happened. That Jesus was baptized by John the Baptist is historically certain, precisely because it was embarrassing to early Christians that Jesus underwent a baptism associated with repentance and the forgiveness of sins.

The material in Mark 1:10-11 causes more problems for the historian, since it does not conform to our everyday experience (the principle of analogy), and because the words and images are taken almost entirely from Old Testament and Jewish traditions. These words and images could be understood as traditional and poetic ways to express Jesus' personal experience of oneness with God and his strong sense of mission. Some features in the Markan account could suggest that the vision accompanying the baptism was a private experience: "he saw" (1:10), and the second-person singular discourse from the heavenly voice ("You are . . . with you") in 1:11.

Theological analysis: The literary and historical analyses thus far have shown that the focus of the Markan text is the manifestation of Jesus as the Son and Servant of God. On the one hand, by willingly submitting to John's baptism, Jesus affirms his solidarity with our humanity. On the other hand, at Jesus' baptism the barriers between heaven and earth break down. At the very beginning of his public career we learn that Jesus is the Son of God and the Servant of God. The theories that only then did Jesus become aware of his divine sonship, or that only then did he experience himself as "adopted" by God, lead us into areas of Jesus' psychological development for which the Gospels do not provide sufficient evidence.

Matthew's account of Jesus' baptism (3:13-17) agrees closely with Mark's account, with the obvious exception of the addition in 3:14-15:

[13]Then Jesus came from Galilee to John at the Jordan to be baptized by him. [14]John tried to prevent him, saying, "I need to be baptized by you, and yet you are coming to me?" [15]Jesus said to him

in reply, "Allow it now, for thus it is fitting for us to fulfill all righteousness." Then he allowed him. [16]After Jesus was baptized, he came up from the water and behold, the heavens were opened [for him], and he saw the Spirit of God descending like a dove [and] coming upon him. [17]And a voice came from the heavens, saying, "This is my beloved Son, with whom I am well pleased."

A major difference that Matthew 3:13-17 shows with respect to Mark 1:9-11 is the shift of the language of the heavenly voice in 3:17 from second person discourse ("you . . . with you . . . ") to third person discourse ("This is . . . with whom . . . "). This shift has the effect of making what is described into a more public event.

The added conversation between John and Jesus in 3:14-15 deals with the question why Jesus should be baptized by John at all. The preceding passage (Mt 3:11-12) established the superiority of the person and the baptism ("in the Holy Spirit and fire") of Jesus over those of John. Moreover, John was said to baptize "in water for repentance" (3:11), which presumably Jesus as God's Son did not need. According to Matthew 3:14-15, John tried to prevent Jesus from being baptized. But Jesus convinced John to proceed by explaining that "thus it is fitting for us to fulfill all righteousness." In other words, it was God's will that it should happen this way, and so John and Jesus should go forward with the baptism. Whether the addition came from the evangelist or the early Church or from the historical Jesus, is not entirely clear. But the addition does serve to explain what may have been puzzling to early readers of Mark's account.

Apart from these points — the third person language in Matthew 3:17, and the addition in 3:14-15 — the Matthean account agrees with the Markan version. And so practically everything that was said about the literary, historical, and theological dimensions of Mark 1:9-11 can also be said about Matthew 3:13-17.

Luke's version of Jesus' baptism (3:21-22) is also basically the same as the other two:

> [21]After all the people had been baptized and Jesus also had been baptized and was praying, heaven was opened [22]and the Holy Spirit descended upon him in bodily form like a dove. And a voice came from heaven, "You are my beloved Son; with you I am well pleased."

There are, however, some differences that fit well with aspects of Luke's theology. According to Luke 3:18-20, John had already been arrested and imprisoned by Herod Antipas. From Luke's account alone we would not know that John baptized Jesus. This chronology reflects Luke's understanding of salvation history, in which John the Baptist belongs to the time of Israel ("the law and the prophets were until John," Luke 16:16) and not to the center or middle of time which is the time of Jesus.

A second difference is the note that before the signs and heavenly voice Jesus was praying (3:21). Luke's Gospel is often called the "Gospel of prayer," because in it Jesus offers special teachings about prayer (11:1-13; 18:1-14) and Jesus prays at all the decisive moments in his life: at his baptism (3:21), at the choice of the twelve apostles (6:12), at the first passion prediction (9:18), at the transfiguration (9:28), when accepting the cup of suffering (22:39-46), and at the moment of his death (23:46). Many of these notices about Jesus' prayer occur in the context of his special relationship with God ("Father").

The omission of "he saw" at the beginning of the vision also makes the vision into a more public event. Luke does, however, retain the second person discourse in the words of the heavenly voice ("You . . . with you . . . ").

This exposition took as its starting point Mark 1:9-11 and showed how Matthew 3:13-17 and Luke 3:21-22 agree with and differ from the Markan version. Following the Two Source theory of Synoptic Gospel relationships, I regard Mark 1:9-11 as the most primitive account, and Matthew 3:13-17 and Luke 3:21-22 as independent reworkings of the Markan source. But whatever theory one holds, the important point is to recognize and appreciate the distinctive elements in each version of Jesus' baptism.

The Lord's Prayer

For most Christians the best known and most familiar biblical text is the Lord's Prayer or "Our Father." It is the one prayer that practically all Christians know. It is called the Lord's Prayer because it was the prayer that Jesus taught his disciples to use. And it appears in every eucharistic liturgy and in most gatherings of Christians for prayer.

Many Christians, however, are not aware that the Gospels contain two versions of the Lord's Prayer. The fuller version in Matthew 6:9-13 is generally used, because it contains everything that appears in Luke 11:2-4 and more. There is no version of the Lord's Prayer in Mark's Gospel (though there may be echoes of it in Mark 14:32-42) or in John's Gospel (though there may be echoes of it in John 17:1-26). Since the text appears in Matthew and Luke only, it is therefore an example of the double tradition and on the basis of the Two Source theory can be assumed to have been part of the Sayings Source Q that was used independently by the two evangelists.

Since Luke 11:2-4 represents the less familiar version, starting with it may help us to see aspects of the prayer that familiarity with the Matthean version may have dulled. The Lukan version reads as follows:

> [2] Father, hallowed be your name, your kingdom come. [3] Give us each day our daily bread, [4] and forgive us our sins for we ourselves forgive everyone in debt to us, and do not subject us to the final test.

Literary analysis: The general *context* is the journey of Jesus and his disciples from Galilee to Jerusalem (Lk 9:51–19:44). The immediate context is the first of Jesus' formal instructions on prayer (Lk 11:1-13; see also 18:1-14). The Lukan version of the Lord's Prayer is presented as Jesus' response to his disciples request that he teach them how to pray as John taught his disciples to pray (11:1-2a). The Lord's Prayer is a series of petitions, and so it is appropriately followed by three short units on prayers of petition: the parable of the friend at midnight (11:5-8), sayings about God's willingness to answer our prayers (11:9-10), and the parable of the father who gives good gifts to his children (11:11-13).

The chief *words and images* in Luke 11:2-4 include "Father" as an address to God, the hopes that all creation will declare his name "holy" and that his reign or "kingdom" will be fully manifest, and the prayers for physical sustenance ("our daily bread"), for forgiveness of "sins" or "debts," and for help during the testing that will accompany the coming of God's kingdom in its fullness.

The chief *characters* are God to whom the petitions are addressed, and the one offering them after the example of Jesus. The *structure* consists of the address to God as "Father," two "you" petitions (for the hallowing of God's name and the coming of God's kingdom), and three "we" petitions (for bread, forgiveness, and help in the testing). The *literary form* is that of a prayer of petition. The *message* is the acknowledgment of God's sovereignty and of our total dependence on God for our needs.

Practically everything in the Lukan version also appears in Matthew 6:9-13:

⁹Our Father in heaven, hallowed be your name, ¹⁰your kingdom come, your will be done, on earth as in heaven. ¹¹Give us today our daily bread; ¹²and forgive us our debts, as we forgive our debtors; ¹³and do not subject us to the final test, but deliver us from the evil one.

The general *context* is the Sermon on the Mount (Matthew 5–7), the first of the five great speeches of Jesus in Matthew's Gospel (see chaps. 10, 13, 18, 24–25). The immediate context is the part of the sermon that deals with integrity in carrying out acts of piety: almsgiving (6:2-4), prayer (6:5-15), and fasting (6:16-18). The Lord's Prayer is a supplement to the instruction about integrity in prayer (6:5-6). It is preceded by a warning against using too many words in prayer (6:7-8), and is followed by an expansion on the phrase "as we forgive our debtors" (6:12b) that links God's willingness to forgive our sins to our willingness to forgive others (6:14-15).

Matthew's version contains the same *words and images* as the Lukan version does. But it also provides a somewhat expanded address ("Our Father in heaven"), a third "you" petition ("your will be done on earth as in heaven"), and a parallel petition to the third "we" petition ("but deliver us from the evil one"). The *characters, structure, literary form*, and *message* remain basically the same.

Historical analysis: In some Jewish circles in Jesus' time there was a lively interest in God's future display of sovereignty over all creation and of his eventual vindication of the righteous and punishment of the wicked. Both versions of the Lord's Prayer beg for the full coming of God's kingdom and for divine help in preparing for its coming. Thus, the Lord's Prayer is a Jewish prayer in its content.

It is also Jewish in form. Jewish prayer is often presented in the form of petitions. Behind each petition is a theology that affirms God's sovereignty, human limitation and need, and God's willingness to respond to human needs. The most important traditional Jewish prayer is known as the "Eighteen Benedictions," most of which in fact are prayers of petition. This ancient prayer is recited three times daily by pious Jews even today.

Why are there two versions of the Lord's Prayer? It is generally held that the Lukan version is the more primitive and more closely reflects the text as it appeared in Q. The exception may be the phrase "each day" in Luke 11:3 that tends to shift the focus from the future "day of the Lord" to the "everyday" present — a characteristically Lukan theme.

The Matthean address "Our Father in heaven" is a common Jewish way to call upon God in liturgical prayer, whereas the simple invocation "Father" is not common. The tendency to expand upon the text of prayers is also typically Jewish, and would help to explain the third "you" petition and the new parallel in the third "we" petition. Thus the expanded Matthean version of the Lord's Prayer probably represents the form in which Matthew's Jewish Christian community prayed it. The shorter Lukan version may have been the form in which Gentile Christians learned and used the Lord's Prayer.

We know from an early Christian's work, *Didache* (see 8:2-3), that Christians were urged to pray the Matthean version three times a day, probably as a rival to or substitute for the Jewish "Eighteen Benedictions."

Does the Lord's Prayer go back to the historical Jesus? Since both versions are Greek and Jesus presumably spoke Aramaic, it is clear that we do not have the prayer in the exact form that Jesus taught it to his disciples. Yet many features indicate that the prayer did originate with Jesus: the address to God as "Father," the hope for the full coming of God's kingdom, the concern for mutual forgiveness, and so forth. All these themes fit with what we know of Jesus' teaching. Moreover, it is fairly easy to translate the Greek texts back into Aramaic and Hebrew. And the theology of the coming kingdom is at home in the first-century Judaism that was the context of Jesus' teaching and activity.

Theological analysis: The chief theological themes in the Lord's Prayer have been mentioned in the course of the literary and historical analyses. God is to be approached in an intimate, personal way ("Father"), not as the Prime Mover or the Uncaused Cause. The content of the prayer looks forward to the future manifestation of God's kingdom in its fullness. In the meantime we ask God to sustain us physically, to forgive our sins (as we forgive others), and to protect us in the testing that will accompany the full coming of God's kingdom.

The Lord's Prayer may be so familiar to us that we seldom reflect on the theological problems that it may raise. The most obvious question today is whether we should call God "Father." This poses a question for those who do not have a personal concept of God, for those who may have had bad or absent fathers, and for those who regard Judaism and Christianity as hopelessly patriarchal.

Another problem is posed by the eschatological framework in which the prayer was composed. Jesus and the earliest Christians along with many of their fellow Jews apparently expected clear manifestations of God's kingdom in the near future. The resurrection of Jesus certainly qualifies as such, since resurrection was part of many Jewish scenarios of the full coming of God's kingdom. But we tend to follow Luke's lead and transform the prayer into an "everyday" prayer ("each day"). Nevertheless, the thrust of Jesus' prayer is directed toward the future "day of the Lord."

What is the "temptation" that we ask protection from? What does it mean to say that God might "lead us" into temptation? In the Lord's Prayer the "temptation" is not so much enticement to sin as it is the "test" constituted by the trials and tribulations that can be expected to accompany the full coming of God's kingdom. The chief opponent in this testing is the "Evil One" — the Prince of Darkness, or Satan. The "evil" from which we seek deliverance is more likely personal (the "Evil One") than abstract (evil in general, the absence of good). In this context we ask that God not allow us to fall but rather help us to remain faithful.

The Wedding at Cana

Reading Synoptic Gospel texts of the triple tradition (the baptism of Jesus) and the double tradition (the Lord's Prayer) requires comparison of the parallel texts and attention to the common and unique features in each version. For the most part, the texts in John's Gospel do not have close parallels in the Synoptic Gospels. John is different. Therefore, though we can apply the same procedures of literary, historical, and theological analysis to texts in John's Gospel, we need also to be sensitive to the rich theology that is distinctive of John's Gospel, and to the peculiar language in which it is expressed.

The text chosen for analysis here is the account of the wedding feast at Cana in John 2:1-11. The story is relatively short and is familiar to many Christians — if not from the Sunday lectionary cycle, then from its frequent use at weddings.

> [1] On the third day there was a wedding in Cana in Galilee, and the mother of Jesus was there. [2] Jesus and his disciples were also invited to the wedding. [3] When the wine ran short, the mother of Jesus said to him, "They have no wine." [4] [And] Jesus said to her, "Woman, how does your concern affect me? My hour has not yet come." [5] His mother said to the servers, "Do whatever he tells you." [6] Now there

were six stone water jars there for Jewish ceremonial washings, each holding twenty to thirty gallons. [7]Jesus told them, "Fill the jars with water." So they filled them to the brim. [8]Then he told them, "Draw some out now and take it to the headwaiter." So they took it. [9]And when the headwaiter tasted the water that had become wine, without knowing where it came from [although the servers who had drawn the water knew], the headwaiter called the bridegroom, [10]and said to him, "Everyone serves good wine first, and then when people have drunk freely, an inferior one; but you have kept the good wine until now." [11]Jesus did this as the beginning of his signs in Cana in Galilee, and so revealed his glory, and his disciples began to believe in him.

Literary analysis: The Johannine *context* of the episode is the beginning of Jesus' public ministry. After the presentation of the many titles that can be applied to Jesus (1:1-51), the miracle at Cana constitutes the "beginning of his signs" (2:11). As such it is the first in the series of seven signs or miracles that appear in the first half of John's Gospel, the so-called Book of Signs.

The most important *words and images* include the characteristically Johannine term "the mother of Jesus" for Mary (2:1, 3), Jesus' reply to his mother's request and the reference to his "hour" (2:4), and the cluster of theological terms in the final verse — "signs," "glory," and "believe."

The chief *character* is Jesus. The other characters — the mother of Jesus, the disciples, the servers, the headwaiter, and the bridegroom — all relate to him and serve to move forward the story that climaxes in the first public manifestation of Jesus' glory.

In the *structure* of the narrative, the first part (2:1-5) provides the necessary background to the miracle proper

(2:6-10), which is told only indirectly. No one sees the water changed into wine. The servers, the headwaiter, and presumably everyone in the wedding party know it from the taste. The episode ends in 2:11 with the narrator's comment, which makes clear the theological significance of the sign.

The *literary form* is that of a miracle story. Since it involves an action (turning water into wine) that transcends the laws of nature, it is usually classified as a nature miracle along with the stilling of the storm, the walking on the water, and the multiplication of loaves and fishes (as opposed to the healing miracles and exorcisms).

The *message* concerns the person of Jesus and what he can do. According to John 1:50, Jesus promised Nathanael: "You will see greater things than this." The wedding at Cana is the first public occasion in which Jesus' glory is revealed and his disciples believe in response to an action done by him.

Historical analysis: The miracle is set in "Cana in Galilee" (2:1, 11). The place is traditionally identified with Kefar Kenna, though most scholars today prefer Khirbet Qanah about five miles away. The time indicator "on the third day" (2:1) does not fit directly with the time sequence developed in the first chapter. Whether it has symbolic significance (pointing toward Jesus' resurrection on the third day) or was simply part of the narrative before it was incorporated into John's Gospel cannot be decided.

Wedding celebrations in Palestine might last several days, with guests coming and going. This explains why Jesus and his disciples arrive on the scene while the celebration is in progress. The customs of having a "headwaiter" and of serving inferior wine near the end of the wedding celebration are not well attested from ancient sources. But they make sense in the context of a wedding celebration spread over several days.

The more important aspect of cultural background concerns the importance of honor and shame in Jewish (and

Mediterranean) society in Jesus' time. Because they ran out of wine, the host family runs the risk of looking improvident or stingy in the eyes of their neighbors and friends. The mother of Jesus intercedes with Jesus to rescue the reputation of the host family. And Jesus responds by turning the water in the stone jars reserved for ceremonial washings into delicious wine.

The image of abundant wine made available to God's people in the "last days" is prominent in various Old Testament prophetic texts (see Is 25:6; Jer 31:12; Am 9:13-14; Hos 14:8). The description of the banquet prepared by personified Wisdom in Proverbs features the following invitation: "Come, eat of my food, and drink of the wine I have mixed" (Prv 9:5). A connection with the cult of the Greek god Dionysus, whose festivals involved the consumption of wine, is less likely.

Jesus' turning water into wine at Cana is described as the "beginning of his signs" (2:11). The Book of Signs contains seven signs or miracle stories: the changing of water into wine (2:1-11), the healing of the official's son (4:46-54), the healing of a paralyzed man at the pool (5:1-9), the feeding of the 5,000 (6:1-15), the walking on the water (6:16-21), the healing of the man born blind (9:1-12), and the raising of Lazarus (11:1-44). These seven signs may have once constituted a separate source that has been incorporated into John's Gospel. Several of the signs serve as occasions for long monologues by Jesus, and there seems to be some hesitation on the part of the Johannine Jesus toward those who believed in him solely on the basis of the signs (see 2:23-25).

What can be said about the event behind the Cana narrative? Did Jesus really turn water into wine? How one answers these questions depends to some extent on one's philosophical presuppositions about the laws of nature and the possibility of the miraculous. For many people there is no problem at all, since they are convinced that miracles do indeed happen. For some others, such events cannot possibly happen, and so the story must be explained on rationalistic or symbolic grounds. For still others, Jesus is a unique case and he (alone) could transcend the laws of nature. This appears to have been the perspective of the evangelists. Others suggest that "things were different then" (in antiquity) or at least that people in those days told their stories about heroes according to different standards.

Jesus' answer to his mother in John 2:4 ("Woman, how does your concern affect me?") has sometimes been taken as a sign of tension within the family of Jesus (see Mk 3:20-21, 31-35). The address "woman" is polite but unusual when applied to one's own mother (but see 19:26-27 and 20:15). The Old Testament occurrences of the question (see Jgs 11:12; 2 Sm 19:23; 1 Kgs 17:18; 2 Kgs 3:13; etc.) suggest a distance between the conversation partners ("That's not my business"). The reason for Jesus' response, however, is the key to the theological understanding of the text.

Theological analysis: Jesus' initial response to his mother's request is, "My hour has not yet come" (2:4). In John's narrative the "hour" of Jesus is especially his passion, death, resurrection, and exaltation described in the Book of Glory — the second half of the Gospel (chaps. 13–20 [21]). And so the Book of Glory begins with the report that "Jesus knew that his hour had come to pass from this world to the Father" (13:1). The cross is paradoxically the real manifestation of the glory of Jesus.

The seven signs in the Book of Signs are at best anticipations of the glory of Jesus revealed in the "hour" of his passion and glorification. As signs they point to the most important sign of all — Jesus' death and resurrection. Thus the Cana episode is the first moment in the series of events in Jesus' public ministry that prepare for the climax of Jesus' mission from his heavenly Father: "For God so loved the world that he gave his only Son, so that everyone who believes in him might not perish but might have eternal life" (3:16).

In addition to the main Johannine theme of the "hour" of Jesus, John 2:1-11 may be the vehicle for other important though subsidiary theological motifs. The most obvious is that Jesus the Wisdom (Word) of God provides the abundant wine for Wisdom's banquet (see Prv 9:2, 5). Some find in the changing of the water intended for Jewish purification rites into the wine of Jesus an instance of the larger Johannine motif of Jesus fulfilling or even replacing traditional Jewish institutions and festivals. Finally, some find sacramental dimensions first in the abundant wine provided by Jesus for Wisdom's banquet (the eucharist), and then in the fact that Jesus' first sign according to John takes place in the context of a wedding, and thus places marriage in a new setting and suggests the presence of the risen Jesus at all weddings between Christians (the sacrament of matrimony).

Conclusion

We have worked through three passages in the Gospels: the baptism of Jesus, the Lord's Prayer, and the wedding at Cana. We have looked at them from three perspectives: literary analysis (context, words and images, characters, structure, literary form, and message), historical analysis (ancient parallels, the history of the text, and the historical foundation), and theological analysis (possibilities and problems).

This simple method of approaching texts can be applied to every text in the Gospels and in the entire Bible. It is a necessary first step in the work of preachers, teachers, and discussion leaders. It can help to increase our appreciation for the literary genius, historical roots, and theological potential of the Gospels.

Twelve Issues in the Gospels

Thus far we have looked at the origin of the Gospels and the figure of Jesus whom they describe, the distinctive portrait of Jesus that each Gospel presents, and the concerns and methods that we may profitably bring to the study of Synoptic and Johannine Gospel texts. In this chapter we will look at some special issues that arise in the course of studying the Gospels. I have chosen twelve issues for discussion: the infancy narratives, the virginal conception of Jesus, discipleship, ethical teachings, miracles, parables, the figure of Peter, marriage and divorce, anti-Semitism, eschatology, the death of Jesus, and the resurrection of Jesus. These twelve issues relate to questions that people often ask about the Gospels. Each topic could be (and has been many times) treated in a whole book. Here we can only sketch the main problems and suggest some approaches to them.

Infancy Narratives

The story of Jesus' conception, birth, and infancy is told independently by Matthew and Luke. Their infancy narratives blend historical elements (Herod the Great, Bethlehem, Nazareth), biblical fulfillments (Matthew's formula quotations, figures such as Moses and Samuel), and theological themes (Jesus as the Messiah of Israel, his universal mission). So successful is the blend that it is difficult or even impossible to separate the historical, biblical, and theological elements. Nor did the evangelists want us to do so.

The infancy stories are told from the perspective of Jesus' cross and resurrection; that is, from what was known about the end of his earthly life. They trace back what was important about the adult Christ to the earliest moments of his life. Biographies today do much the same thing when they recall how a famous tennis player gave his energies to that sport even at the age of six, or how a successful financier was following the rule of "buy low, sell high" as a boy. The point is that what distinguishes the adult was already present in the child. This dynamic is at work in the Gospel infancy stories also.

Most people fuse together the Matthean and Lukan infancy stories into the one "Christmas story." To appreciate them fully, however, it is better to look at them separately with an eye toward their distinctive literary and theological contributions.

Matthew begins by tracing the genealogy of Jesus (Mt 1:1-17) from Abraham through David and the exile to Joseph as Jesus' legal father. The inclusion of four women — Tamar, Rahab, Ruth, and Bathsheba, the wife of Uriah — prepares for the Holy Spirit birth prophesied of Jesus (1:18-25). By trusting God's word revealed by the angel in a dream and by the scriptures (Is 7:14), Joseph makes it possible for the Son of God to be legally also the Son of David and so fulfill one version of Jewish messianic hope.

The second chapter in Matthew's infancy story explains how the Son of David, born in Bethlehem, came to live in Nazareth. The various episodes — the adoration by the Magi, the flight into Egypt, the slaying of the innocent children, and the settling in Nazareth — involve Old Testament quotations (Mi 5:1, 3 and 2 Sm 5:2; Hos 11:1; Jer 31:15; Jgs 13:5 and/or Is 11:1) introduced by a formula ("to fulfill what the Lord had said through the prophet"). They also suggest connections between Jesus and the early life of Moses as described in Exodus 1–4. The spotlight is on Joseph, who guides the Messiah's itinerary by means of dream visions and the scriptures. The Messiah's itinerary, though willed by God, is nevertheless full of death and danger, thus preparing for the passion narrative.

Luke's infancy narrative compares John the Baptist and Jesus: Though John is great, Jesus is far greater. Luke narrates first the announcements of their births (1:5-25; 1:26-38), and then their births and circumcisions (1:57-67, 80; 2:1-40). Also included are the episodes of the visitation (1:39-45) and the finding in the Temple (2:41-52), along with hymns that celebrate God's mercy and saving power toward Israel through Jesus Christ (1:46-55; 1:68-79).

The language of Luke's infancy narrative is thoroughly biblical, using words and phrases from the Greek Old Testament, and appealing to the birth stories of Samson and Samuel for background material. The characters — Zechariah and Elizabeth, Simeon and Anna, and especially Mary — represent the best of biblical tradition.

Yet Jesus' significance according to Luke is not confined to Israel, as Simeon prophesies using the words of Isaiah 42:6: "a light for revelation to the Gentiles" (Lk 2:32). And Luke later traces Jesus' genealogy (3:23-39) back beyond Abraham to Adam, thus preparing for the spread of the gospel to the "ends of the earth" and to the Gentiles in Acts. The tone of the Lukan infancy narrative is one of joy and gladness, with few pointers toward the passion (but see Luke 2:34-35).

The Virginal Conception of Jesus

In Matthew 1:20-23, Joseph is told by the angel in a dream that Mary has conceived a child by the Holy Spirit, thus fulfilling Isaiah's prophecy ("Behold the virgin shall be with child," 7:14). In Luke 1:30-35, Mary is assured by the angel Gabriel that "the Holy Spirit will come upon you, and the power of the Most High will overshadow you" (1:35), in order that the Messiah/Son of the Most High might be born from her. Apart from these two texts the New Testament is silent about Jesus' virginal conception (though there may be hints in Mark 6:3 and Galatians 4:4). There were objections to the idea in some Jewish Christian circles and also in hostile Jewish traditions. Both Matthew and Luke present Jesus' birth as irregular and indeed miraculous. Though representing independent traditions, these two evangelists agree about Jesus' conception by the Holy Spirit.

Is this history or theology? One's answer to that question depends to a large extent on one's view of miracles (see below) and Christology (should it emphasize Jesus' humanity or divinity?). But the historical basis of Jesus' virginal conception need not be dismissed too quickly. In addition to the independent testimony of Matthew and Luke, one must reckon with the fact that there were no expectations in Judaism about the virginal conception of the Messiah. Nor are there convincing parallels from antiquity to the virginal conception of human figures beyond claims of marvelous events associated with the birth of heroes. Indeed, the early Christian claim of Jesus' virginal conception would have caused problems for both Jews (because of its absence in their messianic expectations) and Gentiles (because they might assimilate it to myths about pagan gods). This claim even complicated matters for Christians who regarded Jesus as the Son of David through the legal paternity of Joseph.

The tradition about Jesus' virginal conception surely makes a theological claim: Jesus is the Son of God through the agency of the Holy Spirit. As the preceding considerations suggest, there are also good reasons for taking seriously its historical foundations.

Discipleship

All four Gospels agree that Jesus gathered disciples around him, even though according to Jewish custom prospective disciples generally sought out their teachers.

In the accounts of Jesus' summoning the first disciples (Mk 1:16-20; Mt 4:18-22; Lk 5:1-11; Jn 1:35-42) their response is immediate and enthusiastic. The disciples — also called the "Twelve" and the "apostles" — hear Jesus' authoritative teaching and witness his acts of healing and displays of power. Those who join Jesus "follow" or "come after" him.

The evangelists portray the inner circle of Jesus' followers in different ways. According to Mark, the disciples are with Jesus and share his ministry. Nevertheless, as Mark's story proceeds, the disciples fail to understand Jesus and abandon him during the passion. Matthew presents a more positive picture of the disciples. The disciples are the recipients of Jesus' instructions about doing God's will and about the higher righteousness. Though they misunderstand Jesus to some extent and in the end betray him, they nonetheless display at least a "little faith" and finally are sent forth to "all the nations" (Mt 28:19). In Luke, the first disciples respond to a display of Jesus' power in a miraculous catch of fish (Lk 5:1-11), witness his teachings and actions along the way up to Jerusalem, and serve as the principles of continuity between Jesus' ministry and the beginnings of the Church according to Acts. According to John, the disciples are linked to Jesus in a relationship of deep faith and personal love as his "friends." With the help of the Holy Spirit or Paraclete, they share in the unity, love, and mission that exists between the Father and the Son.

The explicit instructions of Jesus to his disciples (Mk 6:7-13; Mt 10:1-42; Lk 9:1-6; 10:1-12) reflect to a large extent the fact that in antiquity religions and philosophies were spread by traveling missionaries. The demands made in those texts assume an itinerant pattern of life. The disciples are expected to give up their fixed abode and live a simple life with regard to possessions and food. They are supposed to sever their family ties, redefine their family as those who hear God's word and keep it, and forgo the security and protection that might make their journey easy. The very specific setting of those instructions raises the question about their relevance for people in different places and times.

To follow literally Jesus' instructions for traveling missionaries would be neither possible nor useful for most people today. Some of them are clearly time-conditioned. Nevertheless, the discipleship material in the Gospels does remain relevant today. The essence of discipleship according to the Gospels is commitment to the kingdom of God and to Jesus as its proclaimer and presence. The Gospel stories about Jesus and his followers provide models or examples for Christian life in any age. Jesus' wise and challenging teachings about love of enemies, fidelity to God and to other persons, the proper use of money and material goods, and trust in the midst of suffering can be (and have been) appreciated and practiced by Christians throughout the centuries. These core values of Jesus are not restricted to the traveling missionaries of first-century Palestine. Nor are they intended only for an elite group of Christians today. Rather, they are incumbent upon all Christians.

The Ethical Teachings of Jesus

The Sermon on the Mount in Matthew 5–7 is often regarded as a summary of Jesus' ethical teachings. A shorter version appears as the Sermon on the Plain in Luke 6:20-49. These texts contain much more than ethical instructions, and a look at them can help us to understand the relevance of Gospel teachings in Christian life today.

The beatitudes (Mt 5:3-12; see Lk 6:20-26) describe the personal characteristics and actions that will be rewarded in the fullness of God's kingdom, and thus the attitudes and activities to be cultivated in the present. The six antitheses ("you have heard . . . but I say to you . . . ") in Matthew 5:21-48 illustrate how Jesus goes to the root of the biblical commandments (anger as the root of murder, lust as the root of adultery, and so on), and thus show how he fulfills rather than abolishes the Law and the Prophets (see Mt 5:17). The instruction on works of piety in Matthew 6:1-18 — almsgiving, prayer, and fasting — criticizes their performance primarily for public display and recommends that one look to God for the real reward. The wisdom instructions in Matthew 6:19–7:12 concern topics as varied as lasting treasures, peace of heart, prayer, and the "golden rule." The concluding admonitions in Matthew 7:13-27 insist on the difficulty of following the way of Jesus while emphasizing the necessary relation between saying and doing.

The Sermon on the Plain in Luke 6:20-49 consists of beatitudes and woes (6:20-26; see Mt 5:3-12), teachings about love of enemies (6:27-36; see Mt 5:43-48), about judging others (6:37-42; see Mt 7:1-5), and concluding admonitions (6:43-49; see Mt 7:15-20, 24-27). The Lukan version probably reflects the Sayings Source Q fairly closely, and the Matthean Sermon on the Mount can be regarded as an expanded version.

The two "sermons" are best described as wisdom instructions. They move from topic to topic, and present their advice in short and memorable units. Their ethical teachings are set in the theological framework of the Gospels, which present the kingdom of God as the highest value and the horizon of life, Jesus as the model of intimate relationship with God, and discipleship as following the call of Jesus.

As is customary in Jewish wisdom instructions, the "sermons" contain many different forms of expression. There are principles such as "love your enemies" (Mt 5:44; Lk 6:27) and "do to others whatever you would have them do to you" (Mt 7:12; Lk 6:31). There are examples or illustrations (see Mt 5:23-26), sustained blocks of advice (see Mt 6:25-34), obvious exaggerations (see Mt 5:29-30; 5:42), and obscure sayings (see Mt 7:6).

There are also various motives given for doing what Jesus advises: reward and punishments at the full coming of God's kingdom (see Mt 5:3-12; Lk 6:20-26), enlightened self-interest (see Mt 5:25-26), doing God's will revealed in the scriptures by going beyond the "letter of the law" to its root values (see Mt 5:21-48), and imitating the example of God as our heavenly Father (see Mt 5:43-48; Lk 6:27-36).

The variety of contents, literary forms, and motivations indicates that the "sermons" cannot be taken as law codes applicable to all people in all times and places. Rather, their teaching presupposes an experience of Jesus the teacher. They illustrate how disciples may respond to the gospel. They are intended for all Christians, not for an elite group within the body of Christ. They are normative in the sense that they provide criteria or norms against which Christians can measure their attitudes and behavior. They help to form Christian character and provide models for Christian activity. And yet they are not the only source of Christian moral teaching (which also involves right reason, natural law, human experience, and Church tradition). They are, however, important starting points and can serve as guideposts along the way of discipleship.

Miracles

The Western philosophical tradition defines a miracle as an event that surpasses or breaks through the laws of nature. The Bible assumes a wider definition expressed by the terms "sign" and "wonder." Miracles in the Bible are extraordinary events that allow one to conclude that God is at work here. Biblical miracles include unexpected recoveries from illness, reversals in battle, and sudden storms.

The exodus from Egypt was regarded as God's work and thus the great "sign" in the Hebrew scriptures. Prior to the exodus, Moses performed "signs" in Pharaoh's court (see Ex 7:8-13). The event of the exodus itself is surrounded by miraculous events (the ten plagues) and results in Israel's liberation from slavery and journey toward the promised land. At the people's entry into the land, the sun is said to have stood still through Joshua's word (see Josh 10:12-14). But the most spectacular wonder workers in the Old Testament are the prophets Elijah and Elisha (see 1 Kgs 17 to 2 Kgs 13). Miracles were also associated with contemporaries of Jesus in the Jewish world (Rabbi Hanina ben Dosa) and in the Greco-Roman world (Alexander the Great, Apollonius of Tyana).

The Gospels present Jesus as a healer and an exorcist, as capable of transcending the laws of nature (stilling a storm, walking on water, and so on), and as restoring dead people to life (Lazarus, the son of the widow of Nain, Jairus' daughter). In these cases Jesus acts by means of his own power (not simply as a mediator), and his miracles are signs that in him the reign of God is breaking in. Jesus' miracles generally respond to human needs, demand faith, and serve a didactic purpose. Even Jesus' opponents admit his power as a miracle worker and contest only the source of his power: Was it from God or from Satan (see Mk 3:22-30; Mt 12:22-24)? The oldest Gospel traditions relate the mighty acts performed by Jesus to his preaching of God's kingdom (see Lk 11:20/Mt 12:28; Mt 11:21-22). And the resurrection of Jesus from the dead is the New Testament counterpart of the exodus as the great sign of God's power.

Many people (over eighty percent of Americans according to most polls) find no difficulty in accepting the occurrence of miracles. Christian theology contends that miracles can and do take place. Whereas some of the philosophical objections to miracles arise from an outmoded Enlightenment view of the world, there does remain a debate even among believers as to how God works: Does God work directly through what we call miracles, or does God work indirectly through secondary causes?

Current Christian theology looks upon Jesus' miracles as signs pointing to his identity as the one sent from the Father and as manifestations of God's reign breaking into the present. Though they do not prove Jesus' divinity, they do convey an implicit Christology in the sense that Jesus does what presumably only God can do.

Parables

A parable is a narrative about an interesting or surprising case or event taken from nature or everyday life. It refers to some other (greater) reality and leaves the hearers in some doubt so as to lead them to further thought. Thus the kingdom of heaven is compared to the small mustard seed that becomes a large bush and to yeast that when mixed with flour produces a large amount of bread (see Mt 13:31-33). The term "parable" derives from a Greek word (*paraballō*) that means to place one thing beside another. In these cases the mustard seed and the yeast are placed beside the kingdom of heaven in the hope that we will try to figure out what they have in common.

Parables are figurative speech. Some are short (Mt 13:33), and others are long (Lk 15:11-32). Some have a single point of comparison (Mt 13:31-32), and others approach the level of allegory where each detail stands for something else (Mk 12:1-9).

While John's Gospel contains much figurative and symbolic speech, the parables properly so called appear in the Synoptic Gospels. Each Synoptic Gospel contains a collection of Jesus' parables in the form of a parables discourse (Mt 13:1-52; Mk 4:1-34; Lk 8:4-18). Matthew's Gospel presents other parables as part of Jesus' ministry in Jerusalem (20:1-16; 21:28–22:14), and especially in the eschato-logical discourse (24:32–25:46). The journey narrative in Luke's Gospel (9:51–19:44) provides many of the most memorable parables in the Gospel tradition: the good Samaritan (11:29-37), the prodigal son (15:1-32), the rich man and Lazarus (16:19-31), the persistent widow (18:1-8), the Pharisee and the tax-collector (18:9-14), and the talents (19:11-27).

Many parables are introduced by the notice that they deal with the kingdom of God. For example, the kingdom of heaven is "like a treasure buried in a field . . . like a merchant searching for fine pearls . . . " (Mt 13:44, 45). Such parables point toward the future fullness of the kingdom, the inaugurated or anticipated aspects of the kingdom, and the attitudes of hope and constant vigilance that one should have with regard to the kingdom.

For many centuries the parables were interpreted as allegories in which each detail was assigned a definite significance. Though the Gospels themselves provide precedents for allegorical interpretation, such an approach runs the risk of reading matters into the texts that are not there. Modern study of the parables has drawn attention to their focus on the kingdom of God, their use in the early Church and by the evangelists to meet the challenges of their situations, and their importance in Jesus' teaching ministry. Thus they must be read on three levels: Jesus' proclamation of the kingdom, the life of the early Church, and the final composition of the Gospels.

It is possible to regard Jesus of Nazareth as the "parable" of God. While fully embracing our humanity, Jesus, through his dedication to his heavenly Father, his service of others, and his death and resurrection, pointed toward the reality of God and of his kingdom among and ahead of us. His example is a constant challenge and provocation to us to consider what is truly important in life, and how we might better serve God and the kingdom.

Peter

Among the twelve apostles Peter stands out as the most prominent. Simon Peter was one of the first disciples called by Jesus (see Mk 1:16-20). He became a regular companion of Jesus and remained a witness to Jesus after his death and resurrection. Simon the fisherman came to be known as Peter or Cephas — both names mean "rock" — probably because Jesus gave him this name on account of his "rocky" character. Peter frequently serves as the spokesman for Jesus' disciples in various Gospel episodes. He correctly identifies Jesus as the Messiah, though apparently his definition of Messiah needed correction in light of the mystery of the cross.

During Jesus' passion, Peter denied knowing Jesus. Yet, on the strength of an appearance of the risen Lord (see 1 Cor 15:5), Peter became the fearless witness of the resurrection, and continued to be the most prominent among the early Christians. He apparently had a missionary career, and may have represented a theological position between those of James and Paul. Christian tradition indicates that Peter died a martyr's death in Rome in the early sixties of the first century A.D.

Peter is especially prominent in Matthew's Gospel. Peter is one of the first disciples summoned by Jesus (Mt 4:18-20) and is the first one named in the list of the twelve apostles (10:2). When special problems arise, Peter speaks up and asks about food regulations (15:15), paying the Temple tax (17:24-27), and the limits of forgiveness (18:21-22). Nevertheless, Matthew does not overlook Peter's weaker side. In his failure to continue walking on the water, Peter appears as an example of "little faith" (14:28-31). He is called "Satan" for trying to dissuade Jesus from the way of the cross (16:23). He denies Jesus three times in the passion narrative (26:69-75).

The most famous and historically significant passage about Peter in the Gospels appears in Matthew 16:13-23.

Based on Mark 8:27-33, the Matthean version of Peter's confession of faith in Jesus as the Messiah is expanded by Matthew 16:16b-19 to include the promise that Peter is to be "rock" of the Church. According to Matthew 16:16b, Peter calls Jesus the "son of the living God." In response, Jesus praises Peter as the recipient of a divine revelation (16:17), promises to build the Church upon him and to maintain the Church against the forces of evil and death (16:18), and grants him the "keys of the kingdom" and the power to "bind and loose" (16:19). In the Catholic tradition this text has been foundational for the doctrine of the papacy, according to which the primacy of Peter has been handed on to and is continued by his successors as the bishops of Rome.

In other New Testament books Peter appears as the great "fisherman," clearly in a missionary sense (see Mk 1:17; Lk 5:1-11; Jn 21:1-14). He is also the shepherd or pastor (Jn 21:15-17; 1 Pt 5:1-4), the martyr (Jn 21:18-19), the recipient of special revelations (Mk 9:2-8; Acts 10; 2 Pt 1:16), and the guardian of the faith (2 Pt 1:20-21; 3:15-16). Perhaps even more important are the themes of Peter as the repentant and forgiven sinner, and as the witness to the transforming power of Jesus' resurrection.

Marriage and Divorce

In Judaism of Jesus' day arranged marriages were customary. The official act of engagement allowed the young man and woman to meet and to get to know each other under supervision (see Mt 1:18-25). The marriage itself consisted in the respective fathers signing the proper legal documents about dowries and other conditions, and bringing the bride into the household of the groom or of his father (see Mt 25:1-13).

According to the Old Testament (see Dt 24:1-4), divorce was the prerogative of the husband. The procedure consisted in the husband giving the wife a document that stated his intention to divorce her and thus to free her to marry another. The reason for the divorce is vague: "Because he finds in her something indecent" (Dt 24:1). The interpretation of this phrase was a matter of controversy among Jewish teachers of Jesus' day. Shammai understood it narrowly as referring to sexual misconduct on the wife's part, while Hillel took it more widely to include her burning the husband's meal, and Aqiba even more widely to include the husband finding another woman more attractive (see Mishnah *Gittin* 9:10).

Against the Old Testament acceptance of divorce and the rabbinic debate about the grounds for divorce, Jesus' restrictive teaching stands out: "Everyone who divorces his wife and marries another commits adultery, and the one who marries a woman divorced from her husband commits adultery" (Lk 16:18). This same teaching appears in slightly different words in Matthew 5:31-32; Mark 10:11-12; and 1 Corinthians 7:10-11. It clearly expresses the position of Jesus on the matter.

In Mark 10:2-9 and Matthew 19:3-9, Jesus' prohibition of divorce appears in the context of a debate in which Deuteronomy 24:1-4 is dismissed by Jesus as a concession to human weakness ("because of the hardness of your hearts," Mk 10:5; Mt 19:8). Then the positive or original will of God for married people is traced back to Genesis 1:27 ("God made them male and female") and 2:24 ("For this reason a man shall leave his father and mother and be joined to his wife, and the two shall become one flesh"). The conclusion drawn from this biblical reflection is the prohibition of divorce: "What God has joined together, no human being [= husband] must separate " (Mk 10:9; Mt 19:6).

Despite what appears to be an absolute prohibition of divorce, the New Testament seems to allow some exceptions. In both Matthew 5:32 and 19:9 the exception concerns *porneia* — a Greek word that probably refers to sexual misconduct on the wife's part (thus agreeing with Shammai's opinion), but could instead refer to marriage within the degrees of kinship forbidden by the biblical tradition ("unlawful marriage," see Acts 15:20, 29). In 1 Corinthians 7:10-11 Paul repeats Jesus' absolute prohibition of divorce, but goes on to describe the case in which the non-Christian member in a mixed marriage wishes to end the union: "The brother or sister is not bound in such cases" (7:15). So there are exceptions in the New Testament to Jesus' absolute prohibition of divorce.

Anti-Judaism in the Gospels?

The accusation of anti-Judaism in the Gospels is most often raised against Matthew and John. Matthew frequently speaks negatively of "their synagogues." Chapter 23 contains a vigorous denunciation of the scribes and Pharisees as hypocrites and evildoers. The Matthean passion narrative contains a text that has been a source of ideas about Jews as a deicide people forced to wander throughout the world: "And the whole people said in reply, 'His blood be upon us and upon our children'" (Mt 27:25).

The negative characterization of the "Jews" runs like a thread through John's Gospel and places them on the side of Satan against God and Jesus as the revealer of God. In the midst of debates with the "Jews," Jesus denies that Abraham is their father and says: "You belong to your father the devil, and you willingly carry out your father's desires" (Jn 8:44). This text has often been used as the occasion for "demonizing" Jews as individuals or the Jewish people as a whole.

From another perspective, however, it is possible to describe Matthew and John as the most "Jewish" among the four Gospels. Both Gospels are full of Old Testament language and images, and are concerned to show that Jesus "fulfills" the Hebrew scriptures. Matthew most obviously roots Jesus in the history of Israel by his opening genealogy (1:1-17) and many fulfillment quotations. The discovery of the Dead Sea scrolls has shown how deeply rooted John's Gospel was in the terminology and concepts of first-century Palestine.

How then can these very "Jewish" Gospels be read as anti-Jewish? This can happen when they are taken out of their historical context. Christianity began as a movement within Judaism, as one of its several movements (Pharisees, Sadducees, Essenes, Zealots, Samaritans, and so forth). With the destruction of the Jerusalem Temple in A.D. 70 and the loss of political control over the land of Israel, all Jews were forced to face the crisis of Jewish identity. The Matthean and Johannine Christians were engaged in a struggle over how and where Judaism was best preserved and carried on. They contended that Jesus of Nazareth represents God's definitive revelation to Israel and that those who gathered in Jesus' name are the people of God. The negative statements about the scribes and Pharisees, about "their synagogues," and about the "Jews" reflect the struggle in which all Jews (including Jewish Christians) shared in the late first century A.D.

Although such statements are understandable when placed in their original historical context, they should not be used by Christians today as excuses for theological anti-Judaism. The Second Vatican Council (*Nostra Aetate* 4) insisted that neither all Jews in Jesus' time nor Jews today should be held responsible for Jesus' death. It deplored hatred and persecution against Jews, insisted on the Church's roots in Judaism and on Israel's privileges as God's people, and looked forward to the day when we all will call on God with one voice.

Eschatology

In the Christian theological tradition the term "eschatology" has come to refer to the "last things": death, judgment, and heaven and hell. But when applied to the Judaism of Jesus' time and to the New Testament, the word "eschatology" refers to the events surrounding the coming of God's kingdom in its fullness. Then all creation will acknowledge the sovereignty of the God of Israel (the Father of Jesus Christ), and God's new order will be established. The judgment then will be the last judgment involving all humankind, not the particular judgment after death.

The term "apocalyptic" is also used with "eschatology." From a technical perspective, apocalyptic refers to the literary genre ("revelation"), while eschatology refers to the content of the revelation. But apocalyptic is often used interchangeably with eschatology. Or it is sometimes regarded as an extreme form of eschatology, one that moves far beyond the boundaries of history and employs wild and mysterious images.

Each of the Synoptic Gospels contains a final discourse by Jesus that features revelations about the events leading up to the "last day" and about the proper ways of acting in the present. The formal eschatological discourses appear in Mark 13, Matthew 24–25, and Luke 21. There are also eschatological materials in the parables of the kingdom scattered throughout the Synoptic Gospels and in the collections of eschatological teachings in Luke 12 and 17.

The content of the eschatological discourses is at home in the apocalyptic Judaism of Jesus' time (see Daniel, Dead Sea scrolls, 4 Ezra, 2 Baruch, and so forth). The fullness of God's kingdom is certain but future. Its coming will be accompanied by trials and tribulations (the "woes" of the Messiah) as well as cosmic signs and political and natural upheavals. The "great tribulation" will issue in the coming of the glorious Son of Man (identified by Christians as Jesus), who will come as judge and will vindicate the righteous and condemn the wicked at the resurrection. Then God's will "will be done on earth as in heaven" (Mt 6:10).

Since no one (not even the Son!) knows "that day or hour" (see Mk 13:32), the proper attitude in the present is constant vigilance. One should act always as if the day of the Lord were to come in the next moment.

The language and concepts of eschatology are foreign to many people today. Yet eschatology retains great significance for Christian theology. From a historical perspective, one can say that apocalyptic was the mother of Christian theology in the sense that it provided much of the terminology and ideas for Jesus and the New Testament writers. Moreover, it challenges Western assumptions about progress and control, and reminds us that God is the only sure source of security, and that our efforts at control and guaranteed security will never be fully successful. Also, its demand that we live always in preparation for the kingdom can help us to view each moment as valuable and indeed as sacred.

The Death of Jesus

All four Gospels agree that Jesus was executed by crucifixion under the Roman prefect or governor of Palestine, Pontius Pilate. They agree that he was arrested as a result of collaboration between Judas Iscariot (one of his own disciples) and the Jewish chief priests, elders, and scribes. Why Jesus was perceived as such a threat to the Jewish leaders and to the Roman governor is not entirely clear.

All four evangelists focus on the claims associated with the identity of Jesus as a cause for suspicions about him: "the Messiah, the Son of the Blessed One" (Mk 14:61); "the Messiah, the Son of God" (Mt 26:63); "Messiah . . .

Son of God" (Lk 22:67, 70); and "King of the Jews" (Jn 19:3). The "religious" titles in the context of first-century Judaism could well have carried political and military overtones (as in *Psalms of Solomon* 17), and thus conveyed a threat to the power of the Jewish officials and the Roman prefect. Furthermore, Jesus' symbolic action in the Jerusalem Temple area (see Mk 11:15-19) may underlie the charge made against him at his trial before the Sanhedrin: "We heard him say, 'I will destroy this temple made with hands, and within three days I will build another not made with hands' " (Mk 14:58). Thus, Jesus seems to have won the suspicion and hostility of both the Jerusalem Temple establishment and the Roman prefect.

The ultimate legal responsibility for the execution of Jesus lay with Pontius Pilate. It is doubtful whether Jews were allowed to carry out executions in this period (see Jn 18:31). And even if they could, the punishment for "blasphemy" (see Mk 14:64) was death by stoning (see Lv 24:16). Death by crucifixion at that time was a Roman punishment. It was used chiefly against rebels and slaves, and was intended as a public deterrent.

Crucifixion involved intense physical suffering. After Jesus was beaten and scourged with whips, his feet and arms were nailed to the wooden beams and his torso was raised up on a small "seat" projecting from the vertical beam. From the Gospel narrative it might be possible to deduce the medical causes of Jesus' death: hypovolemic shock and exhaustion asphyxia, coupled with dehydration, stress-induced arrhythmias, and congestive heart failure.

The evangelists, however, were more interested in the significance of Jesus' death than in his physical sufferings or in the precise medical causes of his death. For Mark, Jesus' death on the cross was the consequence of all the misunderstandings and hostility that his teachings and actions attracted. It was the fulfillment of his mission as God's Son and Servant who gave his life as "a ransom for many" (Mk 10:45). For Matthew, Jesus' death was "according to the scriptures" — part of God's plan for a renewed people of God. According to Luke, even in death Jesus showed himself faithful to his own teachings about love of enemies (see Lk 23:34), concern for the marginal (23:43), and trust in God (23:46), and thus provided a good example. John presents Jesus' death not as a defeat but rather as a victory — part of the "lifting up" or exaltation constituted by Jesus' death, resurrection, and ascension.

The Resurrection of Jesus

Resurrection refers to the restoration of the whole person (body and soul) from death to life. It is more than resuscitation or reanimation (where presumably the person will eventually die again). And it is not the same as the immortality of the soul (since it also involves the body). In some currents of Judaism in Jesus' time resurrection was regarded as a collective event (involving all the dead, or only the just) that will accompany the full coming of God's kingdom.

Belief in resurrection appears first in the late books of the Old Testament. The final chapter in Daniel begins with the vision of the "great tribulation": "Many of those who sleep in the dust of the earth shall awake. Some shall live forever, others shall be in everlasting horror and disgrace" (12:2). In the debate between the wicked king and the mother and her seven sons in 2 Maccabees 7, resurrection is a recurrent motif. In the controversy with the Sadducees about resurrection (Mk 12:18-27), Jesus sides with the Pharisees in affirming belief in the resurrection of the dead.

The New Testament writers proclaim that Jesus was raised from the dead. That is, God raised Jesus from the dead. What was novel about this confession was the assertion that Jesus as an individual was raised before the "last day." Or, one can say that in Jesus' resurrection the "last day" has already begun.

None of the Gospels presents a direct narrative of Jesus' resurrection. Rather, they provide stories about the empty tomb of Jesus and about the appearances of the risen Jesus to his followers.

In the empty tomb stories (see Mk 16:1-8; Mt 28:1-10; Lk 24:1-12; Jn 20:1-10) the principle of continuity is the witness of the women (especially Mary Magdalene), who saw Jesus die and saw where he was buried. On Easter Sunday morning they found Jesus' tomb empty. And the explanation given for the empty tomb is that Jesus was raised from the dead.

The Gospel appearances of the risen Jesus take place in Jerusalem and Galilee. According to Luke, Jesus appeared to two disciples on the road to Emmaus (24:13-35) and to his disciples gathered in Jerusalem (24:36-49). According to John, Jesus appeared in Jerusalem to Mary Magdalene (20:11-18), the disciples (20:19-23), and the disciples again including Thomas (20:24-29). Appearances in Galilee are presupposed in Mark (see 14:27; 16:7), and narrated by Matthew (28:16-20) and John (chap. 21) in some detail. A list of appearances is joined to the early summary of the gospel by Paul in 1 Corinthians 15:3-8. Mark 16:9-20 is generally considered a second-century summary of the appearances narrated in the other Gospels that has been attached to Mark's Gospel.

The emptiness of the tomb, the witness of the followers of Jesus, and the continuation and growth of the movement begun by Jesus all support the early confession of Christian faith: "He was raised on the third day in accordance with the scriptures" (1 Cor 15:4).

The Gospels in Christian Life

The Gospels are important sources for the history of the early Christian movement. They contain attractive and memorable stories. And they provide the basis for Christian theology. Yet, most people who read the Gospels are not historians, literary critics, or professional theologians. They are either already believers in Jesus Christ or might like to be such. For such people, the Gospels provide spiritual nourishment and stimulation.

How the Gospels affect Christian life is sometimes called "actualization." The term refers to the process of reading and interpreting the ancient texts of scripture in light of the situations of God's people in their present time and place. Just as the biblical texts were composed in particular circumstances and spoke to the situation of God's people then, we who carry on the biblical tradition can and must allow these precious texts to speak to our situation. Actualization takes many forms. The most familiar include prayer, discussion and sharing, and the homily.

The Process of Interpretation

The Gospels are texts, and we bring to them (as to any text) certain preunderstandings or preconceptions. As readers, we are shaped by our personal histories (gender, age, education, and so on) and our social situations (social class, economic position, culture, and so on). Most of us approach the Gospels as "sacred texts," as classics that can and do transcend the historical circumstances in which they were composed, as what we call the "good news" or the "Gospel of the Lord." From the Gospels we expect not only information about Jesus presented in narrative form, but also inspiration and challenge for our lives.

One can talk about the process of interpretation and actualization in technical philosophical and literary terminology. Or one can take a more concrete and practical approach by focusing on a particular text and using it to illustrate the various steps in the process of interpretation and actualization. We will follow the latter strategy.

To give the explanation a focus, we will concentrate on the story of the healing of the ten lepers in Luke 17:11-19.

> [11] As he continued his journey to Jerusalem, he traveled through Samaria and Galilee. [12] As he was entering a village, ten lepers met [him]. They stood at a distance from him [13] and raised their voice, saying, "Jesus, Master! Have pity on us!" [14] And when he saw them, he said, "Go show yourselves to the priests." As they were going, they were cleansed. [15] One of them, realizing he had been healed, returned, glorifying God in a loud voice; [16] and he fell at the feet of Jesus and thanked him. He was a Samaritan. [17] Jesus said in reply, "Ten were cleansed, were they not? Where are the other nine?" [18] Has none but this foreigner returned to give thanks to God?" [19] Then he said to him, "Stand up and go; your faith has saved you."

As we have seen in the chapter above on "Reading Gospel Texts," we must read them on three levels: literary, historical, and theological. This kind of analysis of Gospel texts is essential in the process of interpretation and provides a good foundation for a solid actualization of the text. Otherwise, the Gospel texts become mere occasions for finding in them our own ideas and prejudices. Done properly, the interpretation of Gospel texts involves a real conversation or dialogue between text and interpreter.

Encounters with Gospel texts can open us up to new ideas and help to bring about important changes in our lives.

Since the process of studying Gospel texts (exegesis) has been explained and illustrated above, here we can be brief in the exposition of the text and concentrate on the ways of actualization.

The story of Jesus' healing the ten lepers (Lk 17:11-19) appears in the context of the long journey taken by Jesus and his disciples up to Jerusalem (Lk 9:51–19:44). The journey context is underscored by the beginning of the narrative: "As he continued his journey up to Jerusalem . . . " (17:11). The narrative directly follows Jesus' parable about "useless servants" to whom their master owes nothing (Lk 17:7-10), and precedes teachings about the kingdom of God in the present ("among you") and the future ("the days are coming") in 17:20-37.

The words and images present few problems, though we do need explanations for the terms "leper" and "Samaritan" (see below). The main characters are Jesus and the ten lepers, one of whom was a Samaritan. The structure consists of a geographical note (17:11), Jesus' miraculous healing of the ten lepers (17:12-14), and Jesus' encounter with the grateful Samaritan (17:15-19). The third part consists of a narrative (17:15-16), three questions (17:17-18), and Jesus' final saying (17:19). The passage takes the form of a miracle story (17:12-14) and a pronouncement (17:15-19). For the message, see the discussion on theology below.

To understand this text, one must know something about "leprosy" in biblical times. In the Bible, the term "leper" covers a variety of skin diseases (psoriasis, eczema, and so on) and did not refer exclusively to what we today call "leprosy" (Hansen's Disease). For what constituted leprosy, how lepers were treated, and how they could be reintegrated into the community, see Leviticus 13–14. For other texts about Jesus' healing lepers, see Mark 1:40-45

(Mt 8:2-4; Lk 5:12-16) and Matthew 11:5/Luke 7:22. One must also find out about the history of relations between Judeans/Galileans and Samaritans (who were regarded as inferior and suspect with regard to their Jewish identity for various reasons). Samaria is in the middle of the land of Israel, with Galilee to the north and Judea to the south.

From the literary and historical analysis of Luke 17:11-19, many theological themes emerge. Any one of these themes could serve as starting point for a fruitful actualization. They include being on a journey with Jesus (17:11), the healing power of Jesus (17:12-14), his compassionate response to prayer of petition (17:13), his respect for the laws and traditions of Israel (17:14), how the faith of the ten lepers was tested (17:14), the Samaritan's response of praise and thanks (17:15-16), how the Samaritan "outsider" perceives more clearly than the Jewish "insiders" what is taking place in Jesus' life and ministry (17:16), the power of faith and the nature of salvation (17:19), and the fullness of healing as involving both body and spirit (17:19).

Actualization in Prayer

The kind of literary, historical, and theological analysis of Luke 17:11-19 presented above, can be gained first through working with the text on one's own and then by consulting the many annotated translations and commentaries that are available to the general public today. This sort of analysis can help us to establish the textual meaning and to discount readings that do not fit the literary, historical, and theological shape of the biblical text. It can provide a foundation for the various modes of actualization.

Many Christians use the Gospels as starting points for private or communal prayer. Two traditional methods for using the Gospels in prayer are Ignatian contemplation and *lectio divina*.

Ignatian contemplation refers to a method of prayer recommended by Ignatius of Loyola (the founder of the Society of Jesus) in his *Spiritual Exercises*. Ignatian contemplation invites us to enter into the Gospel scene by using our imagination. We are asked first to read the text, imagine what it narrates, perhaps as a portrait or film might present it, and ask ourselves some basic questions based on applying our senses: What do I see? What do I hear? What do I smell? What do I feel? and so on. The goal is to get as vivid a picture of the Gospel scene as we can. A second step in Ignatian contemplation involves identifying with the various characters in the scene: with the ten lepers calling on Jesus for God's mercy and healing, with the priests who declared them to be clean, with the grateful Samaritan, with the other healed lepers, and with Jesus as the main character throughout. The idea is to develop an empathy with the various figures in the story and to make their experiences our own.

Lectio divina ("divine reading") can build upon biblical exegesis and Ignatian contemplation. There are four steps in *lectio divina*. The first step is reading — the literary, historical, and theological analysis already presented above. The goal is to be clear about what the text says. This step is facilitated by a slow, thoughtful, and reverent reading of the text itself.

The second step is meditation, in which we consider what the text says to me (or us) and to the people of God today. The methods of Ignatian contemplation might provide at this point a help toward deeper understanding. One or several of the many theological themes that emerge out of the exegesis might then serve as the focus here.

The third step is prayer: What do I want to say to God through this Gospel text? Through Luke 17:11-19 I might want to thank God for all God's gifts to me or for healing or for faith. I might want to praise and glorify God. I might ask God for greater trust or for greater compassion toward those who suffer chronic diseases or who are "outsiders."

The final step is action: What difference might this text make in my life? Does it move me to change? Does it make me reflect on my own relationship to God and how I might become more thankful to God, more confident in God's mercy, and more compassionate toward the sick and toward "outsiders"?

Actualization in Groups

Everything that has been said so far about studying Gospel texts and using them as starting points for prayer, can also be applied in a group setting. Many parishes and religious communities have Bible study groups. Some families use Bible texts to take hold of our biblical heritage as God's people in Christ, and to provide guidance in everyday life.

Group study of the Bible can and does take many forms. Some groups use the traditional classroom methods of lecture and discussion. Other groups encourage artistic expressions based on study of a Gospel text. They may take the form of role playing, drama, painting, work with clay, storytelling, and imaginative writing. Any of these formats can help people to enter into a Gospel text and to actualize it in their own ways.

Some groups are especially concerned with establishing the basic meaning of the text. And so they may rely on the knowledge and research of a leader or members of the group. In the case of Luke 17:11-19, text-oriented study groups might focus on the literary analysis of the text, background information about leprosy and Samaritans, and the major theological themes. Groups oriented more toward the appropriation of the text and its transforming potential might focus on the possibilities and challenges that the text opens up. It is best to combine the two concerns, though individual groups might naturally stress one over the other.

Bible study groups work best when sufficient effort and time are given first to understanding and appropriating the Gospel text. With this solid basis they can then proceed to elicit the diverse contributions of all their members. Taken in its fullness, the process of interpretation can help people to enter into the understanding of the Gospel texts and to find applications in their personal and communal lives. The process involves both understanding and application.

Actualization in Liturgy

Everything that has been said so far about studying Gospel texts and using them in prayer and in group settings can also be applied in actualizing a Gospel text in a liturgical setting. The most familiar and prominent actualization of Gospel texts in the liturgy is the Sunday homily.

In response to a directive from the Second Vatican Council, there was developed a new lectionary or cycle of scripture readings. The Sunday Gospel texts follow a three-year cycle in which each Synoptic Gospel is featured in turn: Matthew (Year A), Mark (Year B), and Luke (Year C). In Lent and the Easter season, most of the Sunday Gospel texts are taken from John. The Old Testament reading each Sunday is generally chosen to provide background information or themes related to the Gospel text, and the Psalm serves as a thematic bridge between the Old Testament and Gospel readings. The epistle (second reading) represents a separate cycle in what is really an anthology of biblical texts.

The task of the homilist is to break open the biblical texts for the congregation and to relate them to the eucharist that is being celebrated and to the everyday lives of God's people. An effective homily should contain an educational component that can help people to understand

and claim their biblical heritage as God's people in Christ. It should also encourage and affirm God's people, and where necessary challenge them to renew their lives and to do better. In the Christian tradition of the letter to the Hebrews and the great patristic interpreters such as John Chrysostom and Augustine, the task of the homilist is to explain and to apply the texts of scripture. The homily then has both educational and inspirational goals, which correspond to the two great concerns in the process of interpreting texts — explanation and appropriation.

In the Sunday lectionary, Luke 17:11-19 is the Gospel reading for the twenty-eighth Sunday of Year C in Ordinary Time — early or mid-October in our calendar. Its accompanying Old Testament reading is 2 Kings 5:14-17, a description of the healing of the "leper" named Naaman the Syrian through the intercession of Elisha the prophet. The responsorial psalm is Psalm 98:1-4, which invites all the people of the earth to enter into the praise of God as the proper response to God's mighty actions.

In actualizing this text I want to focus on the theme of thanksgiving. The congregation in which I am preaching are ordinary folk, interested in learning about the Bible and in exploring what it might mean in their lives. In October, many people in the United States are beginning to think about the Thanksgiving holiday in late November. Though originally a religious occasion, Thanksgiving has become increasingly secularized, and the notion of thanksgiving has become increasingly vague for many people.

In my actualization of Luke 17:11-19 I want to recover the distinctive biblical approach to thanksgiving, and to reflect on what difference it might make in our attitude toward God and toward our lives. What follows illustrates how I have tried to actualize Luke 17:11-19 in the context of Sunday eucharistic liturgy. It is presented as one possibility among many and in one style (that of a professor of biblical studies) among many. The richness of the scriptures allows for many effective actualizations and for many different styles of presentation. The content and the style of actualization will depend to some extent on the character and needs of both the interpreter and of the group in which the text is being actualized in the context of liturgy.

Homily on Luke 17:11-19

"One of them, realizing that he had been healed, returned, glorifying God in a loud voice." In this reading from Luke's Gospel we continue our journey with Jesus and his disciples. Along the way we are learning about Christian spirituality: how we relate to God, to ourselves, and to others. Last Sunday we learned from Luke 17:7-10 that we are God's servants, and that we have no reason to expect God to thank us for only doing what God asks of us.

Today's Gospel text concerns the other side of our relationship to God. Although God has no obligation to thank us, we have an obligation to thank God.

That point is made dramatically in the story of Jesus' healing the ten lepers. The healing takes place along the way. Ten lepers — persons suffering from infectious skin diseases and thus kept separate from the general population — cry out to Jesus: "Jesus, Master! Have pity on us!" When Jesus tells them to show themselves to the priests to have their cure verified (thus enabling them to return to the general population), they go on their way. That action took great faith on their part. They at least believed in Jesus' power to heal them. Their faith was rewarded, for on their way to the priests they were miraculously healed from their skin diseases.

All's well that ends well. Not quite. Only one of the ten healed lepers comes back to Jesus to thank God for the cure. And that one was the one least expected to do so — a Samaritan, a person regarded by some Jews as a foreigner, not a real Jew at all. Thus, Jesus asks: "Has none but this foreigner returned to give thanks to God?"

This Gospel story reminds us of our obligation to thank God. Although God does not need to thank us, we need to thank God.

In late November people in the United States celebrate Thanksgiving Day. This is a very popular holiday. It is a day of enjoyment, of family and friends, of special foods, of relaxation from work and other pressures. It was and is a harvest festival. It is intended as an occasion to give thanks for the good things in our lives.

Most everyone likes Thanksgiving Day. Yet, most everyone loses sight of what the day is supposed to be. It is supposed to be an opportunity to thank God for all the good (and not so good) things in our lives.

This is not a Thanksgiving Day sermon. But I do want to reflect on the spirituality of thanksgiving, on what it means to thank God in the light of scripture. The biblical idea of thanksgiving includes more than what most of us mean by thanksgiving. Thanksgiving in the biblical sense begins with the mighty acts of God. It focuses on God's work in creating the whole universe and ourselves within it, on God's liberation from slavery through the exodus and at Easter, on God's sustaining all creation, and God as the ultimate sovereign and goal of creation. Thanksgiving begins with the mighty acts of God.

The Hebrew word for "thanksgiving" (*hôdâ*) means to "confess, proclaim, recite." To give thanks means to recite and confess what God has done in our world and in our lives. In our often narrow and self-centered view of the universe, thanksgiving can too easily degenerate into self-congratulation. We can so focus on ourselves that we acknowledge God's role only insofar as God has allowed us to do the good things for which we congratulate ourselves. This is a silly and perverse logic. Yet, I find myself falling into it, and I suspect that you do too.

Real thanksgiving is the opposite of self-centeredness. It focuses on God and on God's mighty works. It congratulates God, not ourselves. It sees clearly the greatness of God and how dependent we are upon God. Real thanksgiving is God-focused. Real thanksgiving confesses God's mighty acts, not our own achievements.

Spirituality concerns our relation to God, to ourselves, and to one another. God has no need to thank us. But we have a need to thank God. In its biblical sense thanksgiving begins with God's actions in our world and on our behalf. To give thanks to God involves meditating on what God has done and is doing, and reciting and confessing those mighty acts. When we give thanks to God, we involve ourselves in an essential task of Christian spirituality. We proclaim who God is (our creator, redeemer, and sustainer) and who we are (God's servants).

Today we gather to celebrate God's mighty acts, especially in the life, death, and resurrection of Jesus Christ. One of the traditional words for what we do today is "eucharist" — a word that means "thanksgiving." Our eucharistic prayer — the heart and soul of our celebration today — is a prayer of thanksgiving. As we continue our prayer, may we call to mind God's mighty acts. May we approach God through Christ in a spirit of genuine thanksgiving. Amen!

For Further Study

1. *Jesus and the Gospels*. For official Catholic Church teaching on the Bible and its interpretation, the best source is Vatican II's Constitution on Divine Revelation (*Dei verbum*). An excellent survey of the world of Jesus and the Gospels is the revision of Emil Schürer's classic work by Geza Vermes and Fergus Millar, *The History of the Jewish People in the Age of Jesus Christ* (175 B.C.-A.D. 135) (3 vols.; Edinburgh: T&T Clark, 1973, 1979, 1987). The most comprehensive treatment of the historical Jesus promises to be John P. Meier's *A Marginal Jew. Rethinking the Historical Jesus* (3 vols.; New York: Doubleday, 1991, 1994, —). For an excellent introduction to the genesis and development of Christian faith in Jesus, see Raymond E. Brown's *An Introduction to New Testament Christology* (New York–Mahwah, NJ: Paulist, 1994). The translations quoted in this book are from the revised edition (1986) of the New Testament in the *New American Bible*, a fresh translation from the Greek by members of the Catholic Biblical Association of America.

2. *The Four Gospels*. A "synopsis" of the Gospels provides the texts of the three Synoptic Gospels (and John where relevant) in parallel columns, thus facilitating detailed comparison of the texts. See Kurt Aland (ed.), *Synopsis of the Four Gospels. English Edition* (New York: United Bible Societies, 1982), and Burton Throckmorton (ed.), *Gospel Parallels* (5th ed.; Nashville: Nelson, 1992).

The following large commentaries on the Gospels may be helpful: Daniel J. Harrington, *The Gospel of Matthew* (Sacra Pagina 1; Collegeville, MN: Liturgical Press, 1991); Morna D. Hooker, *The Gospel According to Saint Mark* (Blacks New Testament Commentary; Peabody, MA; Hendrickson, 1993); Joseph A. Fitzmyer, *The Gospel According to Luke* (Anchor Bible 28; Garden City, NY: Doubleday, 1981, 1985); Luke T. Johnson, *The Gospel of Luke* (Sacra Pagina 3; Collegeville: Liturgical Press, 1991); Raymond E. Brown, *The Gospel According to John* (Anchor Bible 30; Garden City, NY: Doubleday, 1966, 1970); and Rudolf Schnackenburg, *The Gospel According to St. John* (3 vols; New York: Crossroad, 1968/80, 1979/81, 1982).

3. *Reading Gospel Texts*. The best and most authoritative guide to biblical exegesis and interpretation is the Pontifical Biblical Commission's 1993 document on *The Interpretation of the Bible in the*

Church. A compact edition is available from St. Paul Books & Media of Boston, MA. Further explanations of the various exegetical methods appear in my *Interpreting the New Testament* (rev. ed.; Collegeville: Liturgical Press, 1988), and in Raymond F. Collins' *Introduction to the New Testament* (Garden City, NY: Doubleday, 1983).

4. *Twelve Issues in the Gospels*. For reliable and extensive treatments of the issues, see the following books: Raymond E. Brown, *The Birth of the Messiah* (rev. ed.; Garden City, NY: Doubleday, 1993); Eduard Lohse, *Theological Ethics of the New Testament* (Minneapolis: Fortress, 1991); Rudolf Schnackenburg, *The Moral Teaching of the New Testament* (New York: Seabury, 1979); Wolfgang Schrage, *The Ethics of the New Testament* (Philadelphia: Fortress, 1988); on miracles, John P. Meier, *A Marginal Jew* (vol. 2; New York: Doubleday, 1994), pp. 507-1038; C. H. Dodd, *The Parables of the Kingdom* (rev. ed.; New York: Scribners , 1965); Joachim Jeremias, *The Parables of Jesus* (rev. ed.; New York: Scribners, 1963); John R. Donahue, *The Gospel in Parable* (Philadelphia: Fortress, 1988); Raymond E. Brown et al., *Peter in the New Testament* (New York: Paulist, 1973); Raymond F. Collins, *Divorce in the New Testament* (Collegeville: Liturgical Press, 1992); Franz Mussner, *Tractate on the Jews. The Significance of Judaism for Christian Faith* (Philadelphia: Fortress, 1984); Rudolf Schnackenburg, *God's Rule and Kingdom* (New York: Herder, 1963); Raymond E. Brown, *The Death of the Messiah* (2 vols.; New York: Doubleday, 1994); and Pheme Perkins, *Resurrection: New Testament Witness and Contemporary Reflection* (Garden City, NY: Doubleday, 1984).

5. *The Gospels in Christian Life*. The best English translations are the *New American Bible* (revised, 1986), the *New Revised Standard Version*, and the *New Jerusalem Bible*. The editions with introductions and notes will be most useful in the actualization of Gospel texts. One-volume commentaries on the whole Bible may also be helpful: Roland E. Murphy, Raymond E. Brown, and Joseph A. Fitzmyer (eds.), *The New Jerome Biblical Commentary* (Englewood Cliffs, NJ: Prentice-Hall 1990); and Robert J. Karris and Diane Bergant (eds.), *Collegeville Bible Commentary* (Collegeville: Liturgical Press, 1989). A good one-volume Bible encyclopedia is Paul J. Achtemeier (ed.), *Harper's Bible Dictionary* (rev. ed.; San Francisco: HarperCollins, 1996). More information appears in the six-volume *Anchor Bible Dictionary*, edited by David Noel Freedman (New York: Doubleday, 1992). A good introduction to hermeneutical theory is Sandra Schneiderss *The Revelatory Text: Interpreting the New Testament as Sacred Scripture* (San Francisco: HarperCollins, 1991).